Life's Unspoken Rules

The Guide to Soft Skills for Young Adults

by
Fernando Da Mata

Table of Contents

Introduction: Embracing the World of Soft Skills 1

Chapter 1: Defining Soft Skills 4

Chapter 2: Perceiving Soft Skills in Your Daily Life 11

Chapter 3: Communication Mastery 18

Chapter 4: Emotional Intelligence (EI) 29

Chapter 5: Problem Solving and Critical Thinking 36

Chapter 6: Teamwork and Collaboration 44

Chapter 7: Adaptability and Flexibility 51

Chapter 8: Leadership and Influence 58

Chapter 9: Negotiation and Conflict Resolution 65

Chapter 10: Time Management and Productivity 72

Chapter 11: Networking and Relationship Building 79

Chapter 12: Professionalism and Work Ethic 86

Chapter 13: Integrating Soft Skills into Your Life's Journey 93

Appendix A: Appendix 97

Introduction:
Embracing the World of Soft Skills

Welcome aboard this journey into the marvelous landscape of soft skills! I know what you're thinking, soft skills sound a bit squishy, right? Well, you've hit the nail on the head - they are kind of squishy, and that's precisely what makes them both fascinating and essential. These are the skills that enable us to handle everything that's thrown at us with grace, connect with others on a deeper level, and swerve through life's haphazard obstacle course like a pro.

You see, while hard skills may get your foot in the door, it's those softer, more elusive qualities that will have you dancing through the hallways and into the boss's office for that unexpected promotion. But let's not get ahead of ourselves. Before we start waltzing our way to success, we've got to get down to the nitty-gritty of what soft skills are all about.

If you think soft skills are just a fancy buzzword for 'stuff you're supposed to know but never learned in school,' you're in for a treat. They are the secret sauce, the hidden ingredient that sets the extraordinary apart from the merely competent. They're about acing the art of conversation, making empathy your best friend, and becoming the person that everyone wants on their team. But don't worry, it's not rocket science - which, by the way, is a hard skill, and not what we're here for.

So, where do we begin on this enlightening quest? Let's start with a little perspective. Contrary to the iffy looks soft skills get, they're the heavyweight champions in the ring of life. Sure, being a wizard at spreadsheets or a coding ninja is awesome, but can you deflect an incoming curveball with ease or inspire a group of people to follow your lead? That, my friend, is the stuff legends are made of - and it's all soft skills.

The brilliance of soft skills lies not just in understanding them but in applying them. Imagine being able to read a room like a book or resolving conflicts like you've got a magic wand. Sounds good, right? Well, that's because it is.

Now, I'll let you in on a secret: mastering soft skills makes everything else a cakewalk. It's like having a backstage pass to the world, and who doesn't love a good behind-the-scenes tour? It can take you to places you've only dreamed of and open doors you didn't even know existed. Plus, it can turn the mundane into the extraordinary. Yes, even Monday mornings!

Throughout the chapters to come, we'll be diving headfirst into the essence of what makes these skills tick. We're going to unpack their mystery, give them a good shake, and see what falls out. And you'll see, there's no jargon or snore-worthy lectures here - we're going to keep things lively, practical, and, dare I say, a tad fun?

But let's not forget, it's not all fun and games; soft skills are serious business, too. They're like personal superpowers that can elevate your work, nurture your personal life, and amplify your potential to levels you've never reached before. They're the differentiator, the 'that's it!' factor in a world that's brimming with competition.

We'll talk about how to really listen - and I mean the kind of listening that makes you everyone's go-to confidant. We'll explore emotional intelligence, because knowing how to manage both your emotions and others is like having the cheat codes to life. And let's not overlook adaptability and flexibility; after all, the only constant is change, correct?

As for teamwork and collaboration, well, they're the peanut butter and jelly of the professional world - better together. Then, there's leadership, negotiation, time management, and so much more. It's a smorgasbord of skills, and you're invited to the feast.

Feeling pumped? Ready to turn your soft skills into hard assets? Great! Because by the end of this ride, you're not just going to understand what soft skills are, but you're going to wield them with the expertise of a seasoned pro.

And remember, we're really just scratching the surface in this introduction. There's a whole world out there for each of these topics, and we're going to take a deep dive into each one as the chapters unfold. So stay tuned, because you're on the brink of transforming not just how you work, but how you live, think, and relate to the world around you.

Let's get ready to roll up our sleeves and delve into the heart of soft skills. These are the skills that make life not just easier, but richer, fuller, and infinitely more interesting. Welcome to 'Embracing the World of Soft Skills' - trust me, it's a world very much worth embracing.

Chapter 1:
Defining Soft Skills

Jumping right in from embracing the beautiful, complex world of soft skills, let's roll up our sleeves and start carving out what these mysterious 'soft skills' really entail. Imagine you're in the middle of an intense game of charades. You're not only frantically waving your hands to get your point across, but you're also reading the room, gauging reactions, and switching tactics when Plan A tanks. That's soft skills for you—a cocktail of interpersonal finesse, emotional savvy, and that near-magical ability to get others on board with your ideas. Unlike hard skills, which are all about the technical know-how you can list on your resume, soft skills are the less tangible traits that turn good work into great achievements. They're the difference between a robot and a rockstar in the workplace—and guess what? They apply to every single path you stroll, sprint, or dance down in life. So, let's dive in and start unpacking these essential abilities that'll have you maneuvering through life like a pro, or better yet, like the life-savvy virtuoso you're destined to become!

The Essence of Soft Skills

Imagine walking into a room—a bustling coffee shop perhaps or a vibrant workspace. People are mingling, exchanging ideas, and socializing. What you're witnessing is a live gallery of soft skills at play—the interpersonal savvy that makes or breaks connections. You see, beyond the degrees and technical expertise, soft skills simmer underneath the surface, the 'je ne sais quoi' that often separates the "meh" from the magnificent.

Soft skills, in their simplest form, are personal attributes that enhance an individual's interactions, job performance, and career prospects. Unlike hard skills, which are about a person's skill set and ability to perform a certain type of task or activity, soft skills are about how you do it—and often with whom. They are the very fabric of our everyday interactions that intertwine to form a stunning, complex tapestry of professional and personal relationships.

So, what's the big deal with soft skills anyway? Ever noticed how some individuals seem to exude a magnetic charm that draws others to them, making them natural leaders or the go-to problem solvers? That's the art of soft skills in action. These intangible yet crucial traits help us to navigate through the complexities of human emotions and interactions with finesse and resilience.

At the heart of soft skills lies communication—yet not just any run-of-the-mill talk. We're discussing communication that builds bridges, connects deeply, and opens doors to opportunities untold. It's the kind of conversation where listening matters just as much, if not more, than speaking.

But wait—there's more! Emotional intelligence follows closely on the heels of stellar communication. It's the silent puppet master of soft skills that controls the strings of empathy, self-awareness, and management of emotions. With high emotional intelligence, you're the captain of your ship, no matter the stormy seas of life and work challenges.

Then comes the dynamic duo of problem-solving and critical thinking—the Sherlock Holmes of soft skills, if you will. It allows you to scrutinize issues, patterns, and opportunities with a keen eye, never taking things at face value but diving deeper for the treasure buried within.

We can't forget about teamwork and collaboration. You know, the 'plays well with others' comment on your kindergarten report card? It's proof early on that soft skills matter. The ability to function in a team, to give and take, support and be supported, is paramount. Like gears in a finely tuned machine, we're better together, and soft skills ensure the cogs turn smoothly.

Change is inevitable, and adaptability and flexibility are your all-access passes to the ever-changing theme park of life. With these critical soft skills, you can bob and weave like a pro boxer, ducking life's jabs and weaving through career uppercuts with grace.

Now, about leadership and influence—these aren't reserved for the corner office or those with 'manager' in their title. We're all leaders in some capacity, and our soft skills determine how luminously our leadership light can shine. It's not about the power you have but how you empower others.

Let's chat about negotiation and conflict resolution—because who wants to live a life of constant head-butting and tug-o'-wars? With refined soft skills, you're the diplomat of your own universe, crafting peace treaties and finding common ground in even the most treacherous terrains.

In the juncture of our ever-ticking lives, time management and productivity come into the spotlight. Soft skills help us prioritize, organize, and proceed with efficiency—turning what we dream about at night into what we do by day.

Lastly, we beam the spotlight on networking and relationship building—vital to the realm of soft skills. It's not just about collecting connections like one might collect stamps but about cultivating meaningful and mutually beneficial relationships that stand the test of time and tribulations.

This tangled web of characteristics sets the stage for a performance that can enhance your life's screenplay beyond what any degree or certificate can. Like a masterful painter blending colors seamlessly, soft skills allow you to merge your technical abilities and knowledge with your human essence, crafting a masterpiece of a career and life.

Remember, honing these superpowers isn't some overnight miracle cure. It's a process, like tending to a garden that requires patience, dedication, and care. But once they bloom, oh, how your world changes! People start noticing, opportunities start knocking, and the paths that seemed overgrown and twisted become clear and inviting.

The essence of soft skills lies not merely in defining them but embracing and integrating them into the weft of our beings. As we continue, keep in mind that these are not mere tools for your career toolkit; they are the very soulful elements that will set you ablaze in the market of life. Whether you're a fresh-faced grad or a seasoned professional, soft skills are the timeless treasure trove that, once unlocked, can lead to realms of success and fulfillment you've only dared to dream of.

Differentiating Hard Skills and Soft Skills

So, we've already dipped our toes in the ocean of soft skills, realizing how invaluable they are for just about anyone who's looking to make a dent in the universe. But here's where things get a tad sticky — distinguishing between hard skills and soft skills. It's like trying to differentiate between seasoning and the actual meat of a dish. Both are crucial, but bring very different flavors to the table!

Hard skills are your technical abilities, the know-how to perform specific tasks. Think number crunching, programming, operating machinery, speaking a foreign language, or even baking that perfectly airy soufflé your friends rave about. These skills are teachable, measurable, and you can flaunt them in bulleted lists on your resume. "Proficient in Spanish" or "Can code in Python", sound familiar? That's the stuff of hard skills.

Now, let's switch gears to soft skills. These are the interpersonal skills, the traits that define how you work and interact with others. They're like the secret sauce to your workplace performance; you can't exactly measure them, but boy, do they make a difference. We're talking adaptability, teamwork, communication, and leadership — the elements that enable you to glide through the social complexities of the workplace like a hot knife through butter.

Think of it this way: if you're in a band, hard skills are knowing how to play your instrument, while soft skills are about jamming in harmony with the group, feeling the vibe, and engaging the crowd. It's that intangible magic that turns a bunch of notes into an unforgettable performance.

Now, don't fall into the trap of thinking one is more important than the other. That's like arguing whether it's more important to have wheels or an engine in your car. You need both to hit the highway of success. Hard skills might get your foot in the door, but soft skills are what allow you to communicate, problem-solve, and lead effectively once you're inside.

Plus, let's face it, in today's frantic dance of technological advancement, hard skills can become outdated faster than a teen's social media feed. But soft skills? They're the timeless classics, like the Beatles of the workforce, always in style and never out of demand.

Moreover, soft skills play nicely with hard skills. They're like the dynamic duo of your career progression. You could be a spreadsheet whiz (hard skill), but if you can't explain what those numbers mean to a team who thinks 'pivot tables' are something you find in a furniture store, you're in for a bumpy ride.

Let's not overlook the adaptability of soft skills across different roles and industries. Good communication and teamwork are just as necessary in a high-powered legal team as they are in a bustling restaurant kitchen. These skills travel with you, like a faithful companion, throughout your career journey.

Employers are on the hunt for candidates who pack a punch with their soft skills repertoire. Why? Because while they can teach you how to use their software, it's a whole lot harder to instill a positive attitude or sprinkle in some top-notch problem-solving abilities after the fact.

In the quest to build a dazzling career, consider hard skills as your opening act, your hand to shake at the door. Once you've entered, it's your soft skills that help you to connect, engage, and climb up the ladder. They infuse your hard skills with life, allowing you to navigate the workplace ecosystem with grace.

And hey, let's get this straight: just because they're called 'soft' doesn't mean they're easy — developing strong soft skills can often be tougher than mastering the nuts and bolts of hard skills. But if you're keen to grow, willing to listen and learn, these soft skills can be fine-tuned over time, sculpting you into a well-rounded, unshakably competent individual.

So while you're busy buffing up those hard skills, don't ignore the soft ones. They may be less quantifiable, but they're your silent ambassadors, whispering tales of your brilliance when you walk out of a room. They're the difference between a satisfactory employee and a sensational one; the thread that can weave your name into the fabric of your organization's success story.

By now, you should be raring to go, armed with the knowledge that while hard skills might make up the bones of your professional skill set, soft skills are the heartbeat. Together, they're a powerhouse combination, ready to propel you into a future where your potential is limitless.

Remember, the world's most successful people are often the ones who've mastered this yin and yang of the skill world. They know their stuff, sure, but they also know people. Keep that in mind as you cruise through the chapters ahead, each one a stepping stone toward becoming a soft skills sensei in your own right.

Strap on your mindset helmet and let's dive deeper into the art of soft skills, shaping you into a leader, a team player, and quite simply, someone everyone wants to work with. So on we march, to the tune of self-improvement and personal growth, to a place where your soft skills can shine as bright as your hard skills gleam.

Chapter 2:
Perceiving Soft Skills in Your Daily Life

Let's dive into the soft skills ocean you're actually swimming in every day, maybe without noticing it. Ever had a chat with a pal and they seemed to drive the vibe of the convo? That's emotional intelligence at play. Or consider the last time you found yourself in the middle of a group project. Recall that one person who just had the knack for smoothing over ruffled feathers? Yeah, we're talking about stellar conflict resolution skills. You see, soft skills are like the Wi-Fi of social interactions—silent but vital for connection. They're the secret sauce to acing not just job interviews but life. Whether it's understanding the stand-up comic umpteenth your coffee barista delivers along with your morning brew or the way you instinctively adjust your pitch for a 'please' when you need a favor, you're living and breathing soft skills. And here's the kicker, they can be learned, honed, and mastered so you can wing it like a pro socially and professionally. Trust me, recognizing and refining these could transform your life experiences from glitchy streams to high-def movie quality!

The Hidden Language of Success

So, let's talk about the hidden language of success. You might be thinking, "Hidden? But I'm an open book!" Well, that's the beauty of it, my friend. This language doesn't require a Rosetta Stone to decode; it's all about soft skills, those intangible, elusive qualities that make people say, "Wow, there's something about that person!"

Wake up and smell the coffee—soft skills are everywhere. From the barista who remembers your coffee order with a smile, to the coworker who is always there when you're drowning in deadlines. These people are rocking their soft skills, whether they're aware of it or not. And guess what? You are, too. Every time you navigate a sticky situation without losing your cool, you're speaking volumes without saying a word.

Breathe in, breathe out, and let's dive in. When you're at the grocery store and you let that mom with the crying toddler cut in front of you, you're not just showing kindness; you're flexing your empathy muscles. And when you strike up a conversation with the cashier about their unusual name tag, that's your social skills at play. Aren't you the charmer?

Think about the last group project you were a part of. There was probably that one person who just seemed to glue everyone together. They were both the cheerleader and the gentle nudge needed to keep things on track. Leadership and teamwork, my friends—that's their hidden language of success.

Have you ever had one of those days where everything goes sideways, and you're just there, juggling tasks like a circus performer? That's adaptability. With every curveball, you're proving that you can dance in the rain when the parade gets rained out. Flexibility isn't just for yoga—it's for life.

Okay, but what about when your friend vents to you about a tough day? You listen, offer a shoulder, and maybe some advice if they want it. That's your emotional intelligence lighting the way. Staying cool as a cucumber when emotions run hot – that's something to brag about, even if bragging isn't your style.

Now, let's get real. Conflict is a pesky part of life. But when you can sit down, talk it out, and find that sweet spot of compromise without drama—that's conflict resolution with a cherry on top. It's like being a diplomat in your own backyard.

Have you ever noticed the person in the room who doesn't need to shout to be heard? Their mere presence commands attention. That's influence without the need for a megaphone. It's like having a superpower where your mere suggestions become the game plan.

Let's not forget that friend who's always punctual, never misses a deadline, and has their life organized down to the last post-it note. That's time management in human form. They're basically a walking, talking planner app with personality.

But it's not about blood, sweat, and tears. I mean, yeah, sometimes it is, but it's also about knowing when to lean back, take a break, and sip that lemonade. Burnout is the arch-nemesis of productivity, and knowing your limits is a soft skill power move.

And when you need a favor, who do you call? Ghostbusters! Just kidding. You turn to that network you've been cultivating just by being you—genuine, authentic, and connected. It's all about the give and take, planting seeds for a blooming garden of relationships.

Not to sound like your grandma here, but manners still matter, folks. Professionalism is that timeless outfit that never goes out of style. It's less about the suit and tie and more about the Polish and poise that says, "I've got this," even when your inner voice is going, "Do I, though?"

And here's a gold nugget of truth: success isn't a one-size-fits-all hat you can just plop on your head. It's custom-made, tailored by your experiences and how you handle them. Every "please" and "thank you," every time you keep calm and carry on, you're weaving the fabric of your unique brand of success.

As we wrap up, remember this—soft skills might be soft, but they can make a hard-hitting impact. They're the splash of color in a black-and-white world, the jazz hands of the professional stage. They're what turns average Joe and plain Jane into Exceptional Em and Outstanding Olly.

So go ahead, keep speaking this hidden language, because you're doing it even when you think you're not. The hidden language of success isn't rocket science—it's human science. It's about tapping into the power of being the fabulously flawed, incredibly impressive human being that you are. And that, my friend, is the real road to success.

Soft Skills in Action: Real-World Examples

Many of us move through our daily lives utilizing an array of soft skills without even realizing it. These are the traits that enable us to navigate the complexities of human interaction, build relationships, and make constructive decisions. To illustrate the profound impact soft skills can have in real-world situations, let's explore some practical examples where they shine.

Picture a scenario at a local coffee shop. It's bustling with activity, and the barista is under pressure to serve a growing line of customers. This is where patience, a key soft skill, becomes essential. Maintaining composure, the barista greets each customer with a smile, listens attentively to their orders, and apologizes for any wait they might endure. This simple act of kindness and understanding can turn potential frustration into a positive experience for customers.

Now, imagine a group project in a university setting. Here, teamwork takes the spotlight. Students from diverse backgrounds and with different perspectives must come together to achieve a common goal. By leveraging their collaborative skills, they delegate tasks based on strengths, seamlessly share ideas, and offer constructive feedback. This unity not only improves the project's quality but also fosters an environment where learning from one another is the norm rather than the exception.

Further, consider a job interview, where first impressions are paramount. Candidates rely heavily on their communication skills to convey their abilities and fit for the role. By articulating their thoughts clearly, conveying enthusiasm, and engaging with the interviewer's questions, they demonstrate a level of professionalism that goes beyond the qualifications on their resumes.

Within the workplace, adaptability is tested when a company undergoes restructuring. Employees might be tasked with new roles or learning unfamiliar systems. Those who embrace this change with a positive attitude, a willingness to learn, and a flexible approach are often the ones who thrive amidst the shifts, becoming invaluable assets to their teams.

Let's not overlook conflict resolution, a soft skill vital within personal and professional domains. At some point, everyone faces disagreements, and the ability to navigate these with diplomacy and empathy is crucial. By actively listening to others' viewpoints and seeking compromise, individuals can transform a potentially divisive situation into one where mutual understanding prevails.

Emotional intelligence often comes into play during team meetings where passions can run high. A leader attuned to the emotions of their team members can sense tension and act to soothe it, fostering a safe space for everyone to express ideas without fear of judgment. This capability to manage both personal and team emotions paves the way for a more harmonious and productive work environment.

In our increasingly interconnected world, networking serves as a cornerstone for professional advancement. Attending a conference, for instance, provides myriad opportunities to practice this soft skill. By engaging in meaningful conversations, showing genuine interest in others' work, and offering assistance without immediate expectation of return, individuals can build a web of contacts that may prove invaluable for future endeavors.

Professionalism is consistently demonstrated by those who consistently meet deadlines, present themselves respectfully, and uphold the values of their workplace. Take, for example, a diligent employee who, despite facing personal challenges, ensures their tasks are completed efficiently and to a high standard. Their steadfast work ethic and respect for the role inspire trust and respect from colleagues and management alike.

Time management can be observed in the life of busy students balancing academic, work, and personal commitments. By prioritizing tasks, setting achievable goals, and using tools to track progress, they maximize their productivity without succumbing to burnout. This ability to juggle multiple responsibilities is a clear testament to the importance of soft skills in managing life's daily demands.

In conclusion, examples of soft skills in action are all around us. From a friendly exchange in a retail setting to the strategic alliance in the boardroom, these skills are the unspoken heroes of effective interaction and success. By recognizing their value and consciously developing them, individuals significantly enhance their personal and professional lives, turning everyday encounters into opportunities for growth and achievement.

The world thrives on the smooth interplay of human talents and emotional intelligence. Whether through a kind gesture, a well-negotiated deal, or a leader's inspirational vision, our daily interactions are enriched by the soft skills we bring to the table. It's these moments that remind us of our shared humanity and the power we have to influence the world positively.

Remember, every interaction, no matter how small, is an opportunity to practice and perfect these skills. With each conversation, each challenge faced, and each decision made, we weave a richer tapestry of experiences that not only define our personal journey but also contribute to the fabric of society. By harnessing the power of soft skills, we become architects of a brighter, more connected future.

As we continue our exploration through the following chapters, keep these real-world examples in mind. They're not mere stories but manifestations of potential within each of us. They demonstrate that soft skills, often overshadowed by technical abilities, are in fact the bedrock of effective communication, leadership, and ultimately, personal fulfilment and professional success.

Chapter 3:
Communication Mastery

As we delve into the pivotal realm of **Communication Mastery**, it becomes crystal clear that this soft skill is the cornerstone of personal and professional success. Imagine the power to convey thoughts, ideas, and emotions with precision and empathy–this is the hallmark of a master communicator. Within this chapter, we'll dissect the intricacies of *verbal communication*, shedding light on how our every word can open doors to opportunities or construct barriers we'll later need to dismantle. We'll venture beyond mere words to explore the silent, yet potent language of *non-verbal cues*, where body language and tone sculpt the message our hearts aspire to project. But remember, speaking is only half the dance; true connection is born in the quiet space of *listening*–attuning ourselves to the whispers beneath the surface, understanding not just the string of words but the unspoken messages interwoven within. Mastering communication doesn't just enable us to navigate the rivers of interaction; it empowers us to build bridges between isolated islands, fostering relationships that endure and inspire. Let's embark on this transformative journey, cultivating the prowess to speak with clarity, listen with intent, and engage with the world in a manner that echoes the highest expression of who we are and aspire to be.

Verbal Communication: The Power of Words

As we delve deeper into the heart of Communication Mastery, let us focus on Verbal Communication—the fascinating realm where words can build bridges, heal wounds, or even spark innovation. The power of words is immense, a force that can open doors to new possibilities or seal them shut. It's an art form that, when mastered, can place you leaps and bounds ahead on your path to success.

Verbal communication is more than mere words; it's about the delivery, the timing, and the intent behind each spoken syllable. A well-timed pause can add gravity to a statement, while emphasis on a key word can shift the entire message you wish to convey. To embrace the true power of your speech, consider your words as color on a canvas – they can create a masterpiece or a muddled mess, all depending on how you use them.

Clarity is the cornerstone of effective verbal communication. When you communicate with others, it's vital that your message is clear and easily understood. Avoid jargon when it's not necessary, and be mindful of your audience's level of knowledge. Tailoring your language to them will make them feel included and valued.

But it's not just what you say—it's how you say it. Your tone injects emotion into your words, providing a non-verbal backdrop to your message. A supportive statement in a harsh tone may be perceived as criticism. Always align your tone with your intent, for inconsistency leads to confusion and skepticism.

Embrace storytelling, for it is a medium that has carried knowledge and wisdom through generations. A good story captivates your audience, making your words resonate and be remembered long after you've spoken. Through narrative, you can bring concepts to life in a way that is both engaging and educational.

Active engagement is also crucial. Being an active speaker means responding to feedback, whether it's through questions, nods, or the subtle shifting of your listener's posture. By actively engaging, you show you value your listener's input and adjust your message accordingly. This back-and-forth is the dance of communication, and mastering it is a testament to your prowess.

Persuasion is another key element of verbal communication. It is the gentle art of convincing others to see your point of view without aggression or deceit. Use persuasive language to inspire action and to foster healthy, positive outcomes. By doing so, you become an influencer in the truest sense of the word.

Remember, brevity is the soul of wit. Being concise helps maintain your audience's attention and demonstrates respect for their time. It also forces you to consider carefully the most impactful way to express your thoughts. If you can say it in fewer words without losing the essence, do so.

Equally important is adapting your communication style to the situation. Professional settings demand a different vernacular than casual conversations. Recognize the nuances of each context and let it guide the language you choose. The best communicators pivot gracefully between modes of speech, adapting with ease to the requirements of different scenarios.

Practicing empathy in your communication is critical. Empathy allows you to connect with your audience on a deeper level. It grants insight into their feelings and experiences, enabling you to tailor your words for maximum impact. Empathetic communication fosters mutual respect and understanding, solidifying relationships and building trust.

Logical structure in your discourse is not to be overlooked. When you present information in a logical sequence, it is more readily absorbed and retained. Create a framework for your verbal communication, establishing clear points and connecting them with smooth transitions. This approach not only aids comprehension but also showcases your command of the subject matter.

Words have the intrinsic ability to evoke emotions, to inspire and to motivate. Don't be afraid to use emotive language to tap into the hearts of your listeners, especially when you aim to incite passion or prompt action. However, wield this tool with care and authenticity to avoid manipulation.

Cultural sensitivity is also essential in today's global environment. Be aware of cultural nuances and respect linguistic differences. In a world that is increasingly interconnected, being culturally competent in communication sets you apart as a mindful and effective speaker.

To refine your verbal communication skills, practice is indispensable. Engage in conversations, seek out public speaking opportunities, join debate clubs or toastmasters. Each encounter is a chance to hone your craft, to better understand the impact of your speech, and to adjust your communication strategies accordingly.

Finally, verbal communication can be a catalyst for your own personal growth. As you learn to express your thoughts clearly and confidently, you not only clarify your own ideas but also learn to appreciate the diverse viewpoints of those around you. Embrace the challenge, unleash your potential, and let your words pave your way to a future filled with success.

Never underestimate the power of words. Within them lies the potential to change a mind, a heart, or even the world. As you move forward, carry with you the knowledge that every conversation you have is an opportunity to master the subtle art of verbal communication—your key to unlocking endless doors on your journey through life.

Non-Verbal Communication: Beyond Words

As we delve deeper into the domain of communication mastery, it becomes crucial to acknowledge that dialogue extends far beyond the spoken word. The art of non-verbal communication sits at the core of connecting with others, seamlessly conveying our unspoken intentions and reinforcing our spoken messages. This section unfolds the silent but powerful realm of gestures, postures, and facial expressions that often speak louder than words themselves. Recognizing the subtleties of eye contact, a warm smile, or an encouraging nod can transform interactions, building deeper rapport and trust. Mastering non-verbal cues allows you to convey confidence, empathy, and sincerity, turning every encounter into an opportunity for genuine connection. Immerse yourself in the understanding that each movement and pause carries a wealth of information, and harnessing this form of communication can elevate your interpersonal skills to new heights, setting the stage for success in all your endeavors.

Body Language and Tone of Voice

As we dive into the nuances of non-verbal communication, it's essential to grasp the profound impact of body language and tone of voice. These elements are like the music underscoring a film, setting the emotional scene and giving depth to the spoken word. When your words say one thing but your body and tone convey another, it's your non-verbal cues that are shouting the truth.

Imagine you're listening to a speaker. They're saying all the right things, but their arms are crossed, their voice is monotone, and their gaze is fixed on the floor. How convincing are they? Despite their words, you're left questioning their sincerity and commitment. That's the persuasive power of body language and tone; they can build a fortress of trust or sow seeds of doubt in an instant.

Positive body language is an open invitation to the world, signaling that you're engaged and approachable. Think about a time when someone's warm smile or firm handshake made you feel instantly connected. These gestures speak volumes about confidence and openness. In contrast, negative body language—such as avoiding eye contact or slouching—can unintentionally communicate disinterest or insecurity.

But it's not just the visual cues that matter—it's the way your voice curves around the words you speak. The enthusiasm in your tone can ignite excitement in your listeners, while a calm cadence can soothe and reassure. It's often not what you say that captures the heart and mind; it's how you say it. Your tone can amplify your message or dampen it, painting your words in shades of emotion that resonate on a deeper level.

Mastery of body language and tone of voice is not about manipulation; it's about authentic expression—aligning your external communication with your internal truths. It's what gives leaders their gravitational pull and charmers their irresistible allure. When properly harnessed, this powerful duo can help you navigate social interactions with grace and influence others positively.

So, how do you become fluent in this silent language? Begin by becoming an observer. Notice how others respond to different physical stances and vocal nuances. Watch influential speakers and pay close attention to their gestures and intonation. Self-awareness and observation are your building blocks for refining your non-verbal skills.

Next, practice in front of the mirror or record yourself. Are you embodying the confidence you wish to project? Does your tone match the message you're trying to convey? Critically analyzing your own body language and tone can be eye-opening, paving the way for targeted improvement.

Feedback from others is also a goldmine of insight. Trusted friends or mentors can provide invaluable perspectives on how you're perceived. They can point out inconsistencies between your verbal and non-verbal communication that you may overlook.

Remember, body language and tone of voice are dynamic. They should adapt to the context and audience. A presentation to colleagues might require a confident stance and assertive tone, while a heart-to-heart might call for soft speech and open body language. Adjusting these elements appropriately shows empathy and emotional intelligence.

Body language and tone of voice also play a crucial role in cross-cultural communication. Gestures and vocal intonations can have different meanings in different cultures. What's considered polite and positive in one culture might be seen as rude or aggressive in another. Being culturally attuned means being aware of these differences and adapting accordingly.

Fine-tuning your body language and tone isn't an overnight task—it's a lifelong journey of personal growth. Pay attention to the leaders and influencers who inspire you. Analyze their demeanor and vocal delivery. What makes their message so compelling? It's likely that their non-verbal communication is in perfect harmony with their spoken words, a symphony that captivates and inspires.

We also carry a treasure trove of emotions within us that inevitably seep into our body language and tone. When we manage our emotions effectively, we're better equipped to maintain a consistent and positive non-verbal presence. Your non-verbal communication can then be a powerful conduit for those emotions you want to share, like passion, enthusiasm, compassion, or determination.

In summary, body language and tone of voice are two pillars that uphold the great architecture of effective communication. They can draw people in or push them away, often before a single word is spoken. Mastering these non-verbal aspects of expression takes self-awareness, practice, and sensitivity to context and culture. In sharpening these skills, we don't just speak—we resonate, leaving lasting impressions long after the conversation has ended.

Soft skills aren't just an accessory to your personal and professional toolkit—they're a foundation. Knowing the art of body language and tone of voice will not only set you apart but also pave the way for deeper connections and elevated influence. Take this knowledge and weave it into every interaction, and watch as doors open and relationships flourish.

As you continue to hone these non-verbal cues, remember that they're not standalone. They complement and enhance your listening skills, emotional intelligence, and every other soft skill discussed in this book. Each soft skill is a thread in the fabric of your success, and together, they create a tapestry that is as unique and powerful as you are destined to be.

Listening Skills: The Art of Understanding

As we delve further into the realm of communication mastery, it's essential to acknowledge that while the spoken word has tremendous power, the ability to listen, to truly hear and understand what's being conveyed, can make or break interpersonal exchanges. Listening is not merely a passive act but a dynamic process that requires attentiveness, cognition, and engagement.

Developing listening skills is to communication what tuning an instrument is to a symphony. Without the ability to listen effectively, messages can be misunderstood, relationships can falter, and opportunities can be missed. To listen well is to understand accurately, respond appropriately, and therefore build a deeper connection with those around us. For you, young minds on the journey to success, learning to listen is an invaluable part of your toolkit.

The essence of listening goes beyond just hearing words; it involves understanding the speaker's intentions, emotional nuances, and unspoken messages. It's about empathy, putting yourself in the speaker's shoes and perceiving the world from their perspective. Mastering this skill enables you to engage in conversations meaningfully, gain insights, and leave a lasting positive impression on your counterparts.

Effective listening is active. It means consciously acknowledging and interpreting the information being shared. This can involve asking clarifying questions, paraphrasing what the speaker has said, and providing feedback that shows you are engaged and value what's being expressed. It's about proving through your actions that you're not just hearing, but heartening.

To cultivate powerful listening skills, start by being present. In a fast-paced world where distractions are rife, it's all too easy to be physically present in a conversation while your mind wanders elsewhere. Focus on the here and now, give the speaker your full attention, and you'll find your interactions growing richer.

Furthermore, patience is a virtue when it comes to listening. Resist the urge to interrupt, even when you're brimming with ideas or eager to share your thoughts. Remember that dialogue is a two-way street, and allowing someone the space to express themselves fully can reveal layers of meaning that premature interjection might bury.

Don't neglect the power of silence. Sometimes the most profound understanding comes from what is left unsaid. Listening to the pauses and silences can give you insight into the speaker's emotions and perhaps the points of hesitation or uncertainty. It also provides appropriate breathing space in which the speaker and listener can reflect on the conversation's content.

Active, empathetic listening fosters an environment where ideas can flow freely and innovation thrives. In your student collaborations or as you step into the professional domain, this skill elevates your capability to work with others, leading to more comprehensive solutions and shared understandings.

Banish barriers that hinder effective listening. This includes preconceived notions or judgments, which cloud our ability to listen with an open mind. Be conscious of these mental blocks and strive to set them aside, so you can truly hear not just what you want to hear, but what is actually being said.

In your diligence to perfect your listening prowess, remember to practice regularly. Like any skill, it becomes more pronounced and intuitive the more you exercise it. Seek out varied conversations, listen to diverse viewpoints, and challenge yourself to remain engaged even when the subject matter doesn't immediately captivate you.

Feedback is a gift — in giving it and receiving it. Your responses in a conversation show that you're processing and valuing the information shared. Likewise, invite feedback on your listening skills. Learning how others perceive your listening style can open your eyes to areas you might overlook and afford you the opportunity to grow.

Be mindful of the cultural contexts of listening. What constitutes good listening varies across cultures, and being sensitive to these differences is crucial in an increasingly connected world. Take the time to understand these subtleties and adapt your listening approach accordingly to bridge cultural divides.

Technology, while an incredible asset for communication, can also be a vice for listening skills. The temptation to check messages or emails while someone is speaking to you can be overwhelming. Practice digital discipline, especially in face-to-face interactions, to show respect and ensure you don't miss the finer points of conversation.

Lastly, the virtue of patience in conversation cannot be overstated. The willingness to listen to long explanations or complicated discourse without jumping to conclusions is a testament to your respect for the speaker's perspective. This patience also allows you the time to formulate a thoughtful and considered response rather than a knee-jerk reaction.

In conclusion, the art of listening is a defining element in your pursuit of communication mastery. It's the unsung hero of interpersonal relationships, the silent partner to eloquence, and it is as much about understanding as it is about being understood. Nurture this skill, and it will serve you well across all avenues of life — opening doors to deeper connections, clearer understanding, and concerted success.

Chapter 4:
Emotional Intelligence (EI)

As we delve into the realm of Emotional Intelligence (EI), it beckons us to explore the complexity of our emotions and the profound impact they have on our interactions, decisions, and daily lives. The ability to recognize, understand, and manage not only your emotions but also those of others, stands as a cornerstone of personal and professional success. Emotional intelligence paves the way for empathy, self-regulation, and social finesse; it's where the heart meets the mind, enabling synergistic relationships and effective leadership. Increased EI fosters an environment where creativity and productivity bloom, conflicts are navigated with grace, and resilience is built. It's about harmonizing the emotional with the rational, empowering you to stride through life's challenges and triumphs with insight and poise. Engage with this chapter as you would a trusted mentor, allowing it to guide you towards becoming a more emotionally aware and agile individual, equipped to soar in any endeavor you pursue.

Understanding Your Emotions

Transcending the foundation of soft skills leads us straight to the crux of emotional intelligence: understanding your emotions. This section isn't just about recognizing when you're happy or sad, but about delving into the nuanced narrative your emotions are constantly telling you about your experiences, your environment, and yourself.

Emotions are like a river flowing through our lives, each ripple conveying information about the underlying terrain. By becoming attuned to these ripples, you'll start to notice subtleties in your emotional responses. Why does a certain compliment leave you beaming? Or why does a particular critique sting deeper than others? The quest to understand your emotions is, in part, about seeking answers to such questions.

Consider emotions as your inner compass. They can guide your decisions and shape your interactions. When you feel joy upon completing a task, that's your emotional compass saying, "You're on the right track; this aligns with your values." When you're overwhelmed with anxiety, it might be signaling, "Caution needed," prompting you to step back and reassess.

To start this journey of self-discovery, get comfortable with emotional granularity, the ability to differentiate between similar emotions. It's the distinction between feeling angry, annoyed, or frustrated. This fine-tuning of your emotional vocabulary enables a deeper understanding of exactly what you're experiencing and why it matters.

Yet, recognizing your emotions isn't a passive process; it's active and intentional. It takes practice to observe your feelings without judgment and to understand that they aren't directives, but data. This realization helps you engage with yourself in a way that promotes empathy and self-compassion.

Moreover, the synchronization between your heart and mind is essential. Emotions aren't the enemy of rational thought; they're its partner. By integrating your emotional experiences with your cognitive processes, you cultivate a balanced perspective. You gain the ability to navigate complex social situations and make informed decisions that honor both your logic and your feelings.

Often, people worry about being a slave to their emotions, but understanding your emotions actually empowers you to master them. The more you understand your emotional triggers, the more you can preempt habitual responses and cultivate more constructive reactions. This is not about suppressing your feelings but rather managing them, a skill we'll delve into further in the next section.

Emotional journaling can be a powerful tool in this endeavor. By regularly documenting your emotional states and the contexts in which they occur, you can detect patterns and better understand your emotional triggers and reactions.

Furthermore, practice mindfulness techniques to enhance your emotional understanding. Mindfulness keeps you rooted in the present and allows you to observe your emotions as they arise, giving you the opportunity to reflect rather than react automatically.

But let's not forget the physiological aspect of emotions. Your body often registers an emotion before your conscious mind catches up. Paying attention to physical cues, such as a tightness in your chest or butterflies in your stomach, provides additional insight into your emotional world.

Learning to ask the right questions is another cornerstone of emotional understanding. When faced with an emotional reaction, inquire within. What is this feeling telling me? What can I learn from this reaction? How can this emotion serve my growth? Such questions transform emotions from ephemeral experiences to tutors of your inner self.

Understanding your emotions also means recognizing their impermanence. Emotions ebb and flow; acknowledging this will help you maintain composure during emotional storms and appreciate the sunny days. Emotional resilience is built by riding these waves rather than resisting them.

And finally, understanding your emotions is not a solo journey. It can be enriched by sharing and discussing your feelings with trusted friends, mentors, or mental health professionals. This sharing creates a mirror through which you can see your emotions from different angles, promoting a more profound and empathetic comprehension.

Beyond self-understanding, recognizing emotions in others is just as crucial, which we'll explore in managing emotions in yourself and others. But before you can effectively understand and manage the emotions of others, you must first be adept at navigating your own emotional landscape.

Embrace your emotional narratives, and you'll uncover a wealth of self-knowledge and wisdom. This self-awareness is the gateway to emotional intelligence and the bedrock upon which other soft skills are built. When you understand your emotions, you unlock the potential to lead a life rich with self-control, purpose, and empathy.

Managing Emotions in Yourself and Others

Emotional Intelligence (EI), the bridge between our inner feelings and the outside world, provides a foundation that enables us to navigate through life's ebbing flows. When we talk about managing emotions, we start with the self, because only through understanding and managing our own emotions can we hope to empathize with and influence the emotions of others. This journey begins within, as we aim to recognize, identify, and regulate our reactions and feelings.

The capacity to stay composed and maintain clarity of thought amidst turbulent emotional states is not a skill we're born with; it's one that we cultivate. When emotions run high, it's essential to pause. Taking a moment to breathe and stepping back from the immediate situation allows us to respond rather than react—an essential aspect of self-regulation. This conscious effort to gain perspective is not a sign of weakness but one of strength and control.

Once we have grasped the reins of our own emotions, our attention turns outward. Understanding that each person we interact with has their own emotional landscape can transform the way we communicate and collaborate. It's about actively listening, not just to the words being spoken but also to the feelings behind them. This level of attunement often defuses tensions and fosters deep-seated trust.

Sometimes, the greatest act of emotional intelligence is recognizing when someone needs space. We're all individual vessels navigating our own emotional waters, and what works for one might not work for another. Offering space can be as powerful as offering advice. It's the gesture of respect that often paves the way for effective emotional management later on.

Emotional contagion, the phenomenon where emotions can spread from person to person like a virus, is a testament to the power of mood management. Leaders, team members, even family and friends, can set the emotional tone of an environment. Those with high EI are like conductors in an orchestra, influencing and harmonizing emotions to create a symphony of effective interaction.

Conflict, an inevitable part of life, requires us to leverage our emotional intelligence to navigate through disagreements and misunderstandings. It provides an opportunity to practice patience, demonstrate empathy, and use well-chosen words to turn potentially divisive situations into ones where collective understanding emerges stronger than before.

It's important to celebrate the emotional victories, both our own and those of others. Recognizing when someone has managed a difficult emotion well, or when you've successfully navigated a tricky emotional interaction, breeds an atmosphere of positive reinforcement and encourages a culture of emotional support and resilience.

Emotional intelligence isn't just about softening edges; it's about using emotions to propel us forward. Harnessing emotions such as passion and enthusiasm can drive us to achieve our goals and inspire others to do the same. EI is a catalyst for motivation, pushing us to challenge our limitations and strive for excellence.

Building resilience to negative emotions is another pinnacle of EI. Life's adversities are constant, but our ability to bounce back relies heavily on our emotional agility. Being resilient doesn't mean we never experience distress; it means we've developed an arsenal of strategies to recover and learn from these experiences.

Alongside resilience comes the ability to assist others in their emotional recovery. Sometimes the role we play in someone else's life is to help them find the strength to stand back up. Cultivating a supportive environment, whether at work, at home, or in any social setting, is significant for collective emotional growth.

Practicing mindfulness and grounding techniques can help in managing stress and anxiety, both in ourselves and when guiding others. Training our focus on the present moment allows us to detach from past regrets and future worries, which often generate the bulk of our stress.

Empathy, an integral part of EI, is about understanding another's emotions without judgment. It involves putting ourselves in their shoes and viewing the world from their perspective, a skill that strengthens relationships and fosters an environment where individuals feel seen and heard.

When managing the emotions of others, it's crucial to navigate with care and sensitivity. This doesn't mean we tiptoe around the issues. Instead, it means we're fully aware of the impact our words and actions can have on someone else's emotional state and act with the necessary compassion.

Finally, emotional intelligence requires an ongoing commitment to personal growth. Managing emotions is not a static skill but one that adapts and evolves as we do. Just as we seek to upgrade our technical abilities continuously, so too must we expand our emotional toolkit. It's a life-long process of learning, adapting, and improving.

Emotional intelligence emerges not from a desire to manipulate but from a genuine interest in building connections that are rooted in mutual respect and understanding. By honing this skill, we embolden ourselves and others to engage more deeply, work more cohesively, and live more harmoniously. In the tapestry of soft skills, the threads of emotional intelligence are perhaps the most vibrant, interweaving through each aspect of our lives, colouring our interactions with richness and depth.

Chapter 5:
Problem Solving and Critical Thinking

Embarking on the journey of mastering soft skills, we turn the page to a vital chapter of our development—problem solving and critical thinking. These twin pillars stand as the cornerstone of our ability to navigate the complexities of life and carve paths through the densest of dilemmas. In a world that whispers challenges into the bold steps of our personal and professional lives, the ability to dissect a problem, to view it not as a roadblock but as a puzzle awaiting solution, becomes an emblem of true insight. Through engaging stories and practical advice, we'll unpack the techniques that underpin the art of untangling the Gordian knots we encounter. Critical thinking, meanwhile, hones the sword of discernment allowing us to cut through the fabric of appearances and reach the underlying truth. This chapter lays the groundwork for developing a mindset that not only identifies the layers of issues but also crafts solutions that are innovative, efficient, and enduring. With keen attention to the details that often go unnoticed, we endeavor to strengthen our mental agility, learning not just to respond to the immediate but to anticipate the horizon. This is where your potential meets the challenges of the real world, and with the right approach and a touch of creativity, every problem presents an opportunity to demonstrate the caliber of your capabilities.

Approaches to Effective Problem Solving

As we advance through our journey into the realm of Problem Solving and Critical Thinking, it becomes imperative to focus on the various approaches one can adopt towards effective problem solving. The ability to navigate through the murkiness of challenges and emerge with a viable solution is a definitive soft skill that enhances all aspects of life.

An essential facet of problem solving is the identification of the problem itself. To address a challenge, we must first understand it fully and unequivocally. This involves an in-depth analysis of the situation, drilling down to the root cause, rather than simply addressing the symptoms. It's like the discerning eye of a master mechanic listening to the hum of an engine; understanding the subtle signs that hint at the core issue.

Once a problem is identified, the next step is to generate as many potential solutions as possible. This is where creative thinking comes into play. Like a painter before a canvas, each stroke can redefine the picture. Consider a wide array of approaches - wacky, unorthodox, or even simplistic ones. The brain thrives on diversity, and even the most outlandish idea might be the keystone to an elegant solution.

The process of deciding on a solution is an exercise in analytical thinking. Weigh the pros and cons of each option, predict potential outcomes, and evaluate the feasibility of implementation. This can resemble a chess game, where each move is calculated to lead to success several steps ahead.

Implementing a chosen solution calls for decision-making and action. It requires courage and conviction, often demanding a leap of faith. Like a tightrope walker taking the first step, trust in your balance and focus are critical. Execution is your measured, steady advance across the chasm of uncertainty towards the platform of resolution.

Monitoring and reflecting on the outcomes is akin to the review of a symphony's premiere - it is necessary to hear where the melody soared and where it faltered. Understanding the efficacy of our solution helps refine our problem-solving skills for future challenges. Embrace feedback as a learning tool, and don't fear to course-correct if needed.

Addressing complex problems often requires a strategic approach. The development of a step-by-step plan provides structure and clarity - each phase a puzzle piece fitting into the greater picture. By breaking down the challenge into manageable tasks, the solution becomes clearer, and progress can be systematically tracked.

In the context of uncertainties and unknowns, flexibility and adaptability become invaluable. At times, the path to the solution requires one to be fluid, to navigate uncharted waters with the adaptability of a river that finds its way around obstacles, but still reaches the sea.

Another effective approach is to work collaboratively when solving problems. Engage others, gather diverse perspectives, and synthesize them into a multi-faceted solution. Remember, the strength of the wolf is the pack, and the strength of the pack is the wolf.

Engaging in critical thinking exercises can further enhance problem-solving abilities. Deliberate practice, like that of a violinist's scales, harmonizes the mind to think critically and creatively. Analyze case studies, play logic games, or simply debate and discuss complex issues with peers.

Mindfulness and presence of mind play an underrated role in problem solving. Maintain a level of mental clarity, like a still pond reflecting the sky, to allow the mind to focus and solutions to surface. A cluttered mind often clouds judgment and impedes the flow of ideas.

Another key approach is to always be on the lookout for learning opportunities that can enhance your problem-solving toolkit. It is the sharpness of the axe that makes the lumberjack efficient, and constant learning hones the mind.

It's also useful to draw from past experiences. Reflect on how previous problems were addressed. Each solved puzzle in our past provides insights and strategies that could apply to new challenges. Experience is a wise teacher, and its lessons can illuminate the path to resolution.

Maintain a positive mindset through problem-solving endeavors. A negative mindset acts as a barrier to creativity and can dim the light of possible solutions. A positive outlook is the lamp by which we see the possibilities in every problem.

Fostering patience is essential in problem solving. Not all solutions appear instantly, and some puzzles require endurance to solve. Patience is the quiet companion that walks with you through the brainstorming and implementation stages, encouraging you to give the seeds of your ideas time to grow.

In conclusion, the art of problem solving is a dance of the intellect, harmonizing creativity, analytical thinking, strategy, and an ever-learning mindset. By mastering a varied set of approaches to effective problem solving, we not only enhance our capabilities but also pave the way for success in our personal and professional endeavors. Each problem faced is a stepping stone to greater understanding and capability, transforming obstacles into opportunities for growth.

Enhancing Critical Thinking Abilities

As we delve deeper into the critical world of problem-solving, we find that at its heart lies a pivotal skill that has the power to transform our perspectives and solutions: critical thinking. In a complex world that's constantly throwing unique challenges our way, enhancing our critical thinking abilities isn't just beneficial—it's essential. To thrive amidst the intricate problems we encounter in various life scenarios, we need to sharpen this skill with intention and thoughtful practice.

Critical thinking is a multifaceted tool, a treasure trove of mental strategies that include analysis, interpretation, inference, and evaluation. It's about thinking clearly and rationally, comprehending the logical connection between ideas, and not taking information at face value. To enhance our critical thinking, we need to delve beyond surface level and ask probing questions. Why is this the way it is? What evidence supports this claim? What conclusions can be logically drawn from the facts at hand?

To strengthen our critical thinking muscles, we must first adopt an attitude of curiosity. This curiosity drives us to explore ideas deeply rather than just accepting them. It prompts us to investigate further, to seek out diverse sources of information and to remain open-minded to new perspectives—even when they challenge our pre-conceived notions.

The foundation of strong critical thinking lies in the art of reflecting critically on our thought processes. It's about engaging in metacognition, or thinking about thinking. By stepping back to examine our own beliefs, assumptions, and biases, we can start to pinpoint where our reasoning may go astray. Such self-examination illuminates how our thoughts are formed or influenced, paving the way for more objective and balanced thinking.

Another essential element in bolstering critical thinking is effective communication. Clear communication of our ideas and understanding others' perspectives is important in refining thought processes. It's a collaborative effort, where feedback serves as the crucible for refining ideas and arguments. Actively listening and engaging in respectful discourse can expose the strengths and weaknesses in various lines of reasoning.

Enhancing critical thinking abilities also involves practicing problem-solving in a structured manner. Start by clearly defining the problem at hand; then gather relevant information and assess it critically. Weigh the credibility of the sources and the validity of the data. Formulating possible solutions requires creativity, but evaluating those options must be done methodically and logically. This blend of creativity and logic is a hallmark of critical thinking prowess.

To sharpen analytical skills, make a practice of dissecting complex ideas into smaller, more manageable parts. Analyze how these parts relate to one another and to the whole. By breaking down information, you become more adept at identifying underlying assumptions and constructing logical arguments that draw upon interrelated concepts. This process also aids in reducing the complexity of problems, making them more digestible.

As you refine your critical thinking, it's crucial to develop reasoning skills. Assess the implications of arguments and the consequences of actions. Evaluate logic, spot fallacies in reasoning, and avoid being persuaded by rhetoric that lacks substance. Thinking critically means being able to construct and deconstruct arguments, discerning truth from falsehood and wisdom from mere information.

When it comes to cultivating critical thinking, there is no substitute for practice. It's an ongoing process that requires consistent and deliberate effort. Engage with challenging texts, participate in debates, solve puzzles, and take on problems that stretch your cognitive boundaries. Each of these activities hones your ability to apply critical thinking in a variety of contexts.

It's also key to extend this practice beyond intellectual exercises and into the realm of everyday life. Critical thinking should inform our daily decisions, from the mundane to the major. Whether it's interpreting news articles, making financial choices, or planning our career paths, critical thinking helps us navigate life with a more discerning and empowered approach.

Learning from others can significantly enhance our critical thinking. Observing how experienced problem solvers dissect issues, ask penetrating questions, and articulate their thought process is incredibly beneficial. It provides a model that we can adapt and apply to our own challenges. Mentorship, in particular, can be a powerhouse for transferring such knowledge and skills.

While practicing critical thinking, it's important to cultivate intellectual humility. Acknowledge the limits of your knowledge and be willing to adjust your views when presented with new evidence or better reasoning. This openness to learning is a trait of those who think critically—it keeps the mind nimble and responsive to the ever-evolving landscape of ideas.

In the pursuit of mastering critical thinking, incorporating perspectives from a wide range of disciplines and cultures enriches our understanding. Embracing diversity in thought and approach can offer alternative angles and innovative solutions that might otherwise be overlooked. Remember, great ideas don't exist in a vacuum—they're often the result of collaborative and multi-faceted exploration.

Lastly, critical thinking thrives in an environment that encourages challenge and supports intellectual risk-taking. Engage in environments where your ideas can be tested, where debate and discussion are welcomed, and where it's safe to make—and learn from—mistakes. It is through this iterative process of trial and error that our critical faculties are sharpened, and our solutions are refined.

As you continue this journey, remember that enhancing your critical thinking abilities is a powerful investment in yourself. It will serve you in countless ways, from your academic pursuits to your personal lives, from your professional endeavors to your civic engagements. It's a skill that not only solves problems but also enriches the very fabric of our understanding. Embrace the challenge, elevate your thinking, and watch as doors of opportunity swing wide open before you.

Chapter 6:
Teamwork and Collaboration

In the symphony of success, each section—be it the harmonious flow of communication, the resonant chords of emotional intelligence, or the intricate melodies of problem-solving—prepares us for the crescendo that is teamwork and collaboration. As we turn the page to this vibrant chapter, we delve into the dynamics of teamwork where, like a conductor, we learn to unify diverse individuals with distinct roles into an orchestra delivering a flawless performance. Equipped with the baton of leadership, we explore ways to nurture collaborative environments where ideas resonate in unison, fostering innovation and creating solutions that resonate beyond the sum of their parts. By mastering this art, we don't just contribute; we amplify the skills and passions of those around us, crafting a legacy of harmonious achievement and collective brilliance.

The Dynamics of Teamwork

Stepping into the realm of teamwork, we engage with a vibrant tapestry of individual talents, personalities, and perspectives harmoniously woven together. The dynamics of teamwork are akin to the inner workings of a clock – each gear, though distinct and with a different role, is pivotal to the mechanism's success.

The power of teamwork lies not just in bringing people together, but in uniting them towards a common goal. It is about striking a balance between individual autonomy and collective responsibility, a subtle yet intricate dance where every step counts and every dancer depends on the rhythm of the other.

Let us consider the concept of synergy, wherein the sum of a team's efforts exceeds the capabilities of its individual members. Synergy isn't just a buzzword; it is the lifeblood of effective teams. A group harnessing synergy finds itself accomplishing more, with less strain and more enjoyment. This is the magnum opus of teamwork – to forge a bond that transforms solitary sparks into a roaring fire of productivity and innovation.

It's essential to recognize that teams are ever-evolving entities. The dynamics shift as projects progress, goals are redefined, and members grow. A team that adapts, channels each member's strength, and shores up weaknesses stands resilient against the currents of change and challenges. As roles shift and tasks are reassigned, everyone should remain nimble, willing to step into the breach or step back when needed.

To foster positive team dynamics, communication must be held sacrosanct. Open, honest, and clear communication builds trust, mitigates conflict, and paves the way for creative collaboration. Remember, it is not merely about speaking up, but also about being an active listener, attuned to the undercurrents of verbal and non-verbal cues alike.

Conflict, while often perceived as a harbinger of discord, can in fact be a catalyst for growth. When approached constructively, it can unravel misunderstandings, broaden perspectives, and reinforce bonds. The art lies not in avoiding conflict but in harnessing it as a tool for team development and collective problem-solving.

Diversity within teams is a beacon of strength. It encourages multifaceted thinking and nurtures an environment where innovation thrives. Each member brings their unique worldview, experiences, and skills to the fore, creating a mosaic of insights that can address complex issues with a panoply of solutions.

Leadership within teams doesn't always come with a title. It often emerges organically, with individuals stepping forward, taking initiative, and guiding the collective towards its objectives. This fluid form of leadership is instrumental in empowering each member, fostering a sense of ownership and commitment to the team's success.

Motivation within teams is multifaceted. It springs not only from individual drives but also the shared passion for a project's success. Celebrating both collective achievements and individual contributions stokes the embers of motivation, inspiring team members to continue pushing boundaries.

Accountability is the psychological glue that holds a team together. When members hold themselves and each other responsible for their parts, they develop a mutual respect that is the foundation of a high-functioning team. Establishing clear expectations and consequences fosters an environment of reliability and trust. This isn't about punishment, it's about responsibility to oneself and the group.

Teamwork nourishes personal and professional growth. Working alongside others, we are presented with opportunities to learn, teach, and refine our skills. Teams are the incubators for leadership, patience, resilience, and a plethora of soft skills that transcend the workplace, enriching every aspect of life.

What's more, camaraderie and support networks born from teamwork can mitigate the stresses inherent in challenging projects. Knowing you have a collective ready to provide support and expertise can reduce feelings of isolation and amplify the joy found in working collaboratively.

Indeed, the dynamics of teamwork are a delicate balance, one that requires conscious effort, genuine empathy, and a steadfast commitment to common objectives. It calls for both the celebration of individuality and the embrace of togetherness. It is where humility meets confidence, and learning intersects with leading.

In closing, we must always be mindful that teams are, at their core, human. They thrive on connection, understanding, and respect. Our shared humanity is the ultimate bond, and when nurtured within a team, it becomes the cornerstone of unimaginable achievements and shared success. As we dive deeper into the facets of nurturing collaborative environments, keep the principles of teamwork dynamics close; they are the winds that will sail us to the shores of our greatest potential.

Thus, the dynamics of teamwork challenge us to rise above our own limitations, to aspire for more collaboratively than we could ever do alone. As we cultivate these dynamic bonds and foster an ecosystem of mutual support, our teams transform into more than just groups of individuals—they become a united front that is resilient, innovative, and exceptional in every endeavor undertaken.

Nurturing Collaborative Environments

In the symphony of teamwork, every note, each player, and the collective harmony matter. As we explore the vibrant realm of Nurturing Collaborative Environments, we are effectively opening doors to manifold opportunities for learning, innovation, and growth. Like gardeners who recognize that the most beautiful blooms come from plants that thrive together, we too can cultivate environments where collaboration is as natural as breathing.

A collaborative environment is not just about working alongside each other—it's about fostering a climate of support, trust, and mutual respect. Envision a workspace where ideas are exchanged freely, where the winds of creativity fuel the spirit of joint endeavor. To nurture such a fertile ground, it is essential to understand the pillars that uphold it.

Communication is the lifeblood of any collaborative environment. It's not just about talking; it's about conversing with intention, listening actively, and creating an open dialogue where thoughts can be expressed without fear of judgment. The most harmonious teams are those that have mastered the art of communication, sowing seeds for trust to flourish.

Importantly, embracing diversity in all its forms—thought, experience, culture, and beyond—is vital. Diversity sparks creativity and drives innovation. By valuing each team member's unique contributions, we weave a stronger, more resilient fabric for our collaborative tapestry.

Establishing clear goals is akin to mapping the journey for a treasure hunt. It charts the course and ensures everyone is aligned towards the same horizon. Goals provide purpose and a sense of shared destiny, allowing each member to see how their effort contributes to the greater mosaic of success.

Encouraging autonomy while maintaining a sense of unity can feel like walking a tightrope. Yet, it's essential for nurturing a collaborative environment. Empowering team members to take ownership of their work not only fosters responsibility but also ignites passion, as they become intrinsically motivated by their contributions to the team's vision.

Recognizing and celebrating successes, whether they're small milestones or major achievements, amplifies positive reinforcement and galvanizes the team spirit. It's an acknowledgment that every member has played an instrumental role in reaching new heights.

Conflict, though often seen as a negative force, can be a crucible for growth when navigated thoughtfully. In a truly collaborative environment, differences are addressed openly and constructively, with an emphasis on finding mutual solutions that propel the team forward.

Creating a supportive atmosphere cannot be understated. Constructive feedback, mentorship opportunities, and resources for professional development are the nutrients that sustain a collaborative environment. When individuals feel their growth is nurtured, their commitment to the team's purpose deepens in turn.

Accessibility is a cornerstone of collaboration. This means ensuring that everyone has access to the tools, information, and people they need to be successful. When the gates of opportunity are open to all, the chances for collective success skyrocket.

Maintaining a work-life balance is essential not only for individual well-being but also for the health of the team. A burnt-out team can hardly collaborate effectively. Recognizing the value of time for rest and rejuvenation can lead to a more energized and creative collaboration.

The physical environment too plays a critical role in fostering collaboration. Spaces that encourage serendipitous interactions, creative brainstorming and quiet reflection can greatly enhance the collaborative spirit.

Adopting a mindset that values collaboration over individual heroism is a fundamental shift that can revolutionize the way we work. When the team's success becomes the ultimate goal, silos break down, and a unified front emerges to tackle challenges with gusto.

Finally, leading by example is perhaps the most potent way to nurture a collaborative environment. When leaders roll up their sleeves and join in the effort, a message is sent that collaboration is not just a concept, but a living, breathing culture within the organization or group.

In essence, nurturing a collaborative environment is a continual process of planting, watering, and tending to the garden of teamwork. It requires patience, dedication, and the belief that the sum is indeed greater than its parts. As we commit to these principles, we cultivate a space where not only do ideas blossom but also where individuals grow alongside each other, creating an interwoven story of shared success.

In the end, it's about creating a legacy of collaboration that outlives individual projects and leaves an indelible imprint on the hearts and minds of all its participants. This is the magic of a collaborative environment: it transforms groups of people into communities of innovators, learners, and leaders, united in their quest for excellence.

Chapter 7:
Adaptability and Flexibility

In a world that's changing at an unprecedented pace, the ability to pivot and gracefully handle the unexpected has become an invaluable asset. Chapter 7 delves into the heart of **Adaptability and Flexibility**, essential soft skills that empower you to withstand and thrive amid the inevitable shifts life throws your way. As you've grown through communication mastery, emotional intelligence, problem-solving, and honed your ability to work well with others, you'll now learn that embracing change isn't merely about survival; it's about seeking out opportunities to learn, grow, and expand your horizons. We navigate through the significance of being adaptable and flexible, reinforcing that these are not inborn traits but skills that can be cultivated with intention and practice. It's about making a conscious decision to stay nimble in your thinking and actions, to not just ride the waves of change but to catch them, to surf towards a horizon of possibility. You'll explore how flexibility enables you to pivot without fear and adaptability allows you to reinvent yourself, your methods, and even your goals as circumstances evolve. Through these pages, we're not just aiming to equip you with the capability to adjust your sails amidst the winds of change but to do so with a spirit that remains unshaken and eyes that are always scanning for the silver lining.

Embracing Change

In the landscape of life, change is the only constant. One might say that change carries with it the seeds of growth, a quintessential element for the nourishment of adaptability and flexibility. To thrive, not just survive, we must open our arms to the shifting sands of our personal and professional worlds.

Embracing change begins with an awareness—an understanding that what is here today may evolve or disappear tomorrow. It is a dance with uncertainty, where the music's tempo can quicken without notice. Students and young adults stand at a pivotal stage where the winds of change are both a test and an invitation to grow.

Navigating change requires resilience, a quality that allows us to rebound from setbacks and forge ahead with renewed vigor. The path of change is strewn with obstacles, yet these very hurdles sculpt our character, imbuing us with strength and wisdom. The beauty lies not in the permanence of our circumstances but in our ability to adapt and flourish despite them.

Consider change as a catalyst for innovation. When we release our grip on the old, we make room for new ideas and creative solutions. The sparks of invention are fanned by the need to adjust and to view the familiar through a different lens. Young minds are fertile grounds for such innovation, as their adaptability is often untainted by the shackles of 'the way things have always been done.'

Embracing change also entails letting go of fear. It is fear that roots us in comfort zones and whispers doubts into our convictions about moving forward. However, when we step beyond the edge of the known, we learn to trust in our ability to face the unknown. It is in the unknown that potential lies coiled, like a spring waiting to be released.

The value of adaptability is palpable in today's fast-paced world. Industries and technologies advance at a breakneck speed, demanding that we keep pace or risk being left behind. Embracing change means staying curious, continuously learning, and remaining open to new experiences. Each new experience is an opportunity to gain fresh insights and broaden one's horizons.

We must also recognize that change can be a process rather than an event. Some changes are abrupt, but many evolve over time. Developing the patience to see the journey through, even when the destination isn't immediate, stands at the heart of adaptability.

To be truly flexible is to understand that there are numerous ways to reach an outcome. It involves breaking down the walls of 'either-or' thinking and realizing that multiple paths can lead to success. This flexible outlook enables individuals to pivot when a chosen path is blocked, finding alternative routes to their goals.

Furthermore, embracing change means developing an open-minded attitude. Preconceived notions and biases can prevent us from fully diving into new perspectives and possibilities. By fostering an attitude of openness, we allow ourselves to take in diverse viewpoints, which can enrich our understanding and lead to greater personal growth.

Embracing change is also about preparation. While we cannot predict every turn in the road, we can equip ourselves with a toolkit of soft skills—such as communication, emotional intelligence, and problem-solving—that enable us to navigate the unpredictable. These skills are the lifeboat that keeps us afloat when the tide of change seeks to upend us.

Change often invites collaboration. No one is an island, and facing change collectively can tap into the collective strength of teams and communities. Much like a flock of birds adjusting to a new wind pattern, there is power in numbers and shared experience. Here, adaptability and flexibility become not just personal traits but a synergistic force.

In a world where change is inevitable, it's our response to it that defines our journey. A proactive stance towards change positions us as architects of our destiny, shaping our paths with intention and foresight. We can choose to see change as an adversary or an ally on our road to success.

Societal advancements are largely driven by those who have taken Change by the hand and walked boldly into the future. History is dotted with stories of individuals and societies that accepted the challenge of change, turning uncertainties into stepping stones for progress.

In conclusion, embracing change is a vital soft skill, one that intertwines with every aspect of adaptability and flexibility. As we continually evolve and journey through the various stages of our lives, remember that it is our capacity to embrace change that will ultimately determine the richness of our personal and professional tapestries.

The secret to thriving in a world saturated with change is not in discovering a foolproof way to avoid it but in learning to ride its waves with grace and determination. Through this, students and young adults can craft a future marked not by fear of the unknown but by the anticipation of the potential that each new change brings.

Developing a Growth Mindset

In the previous chapter, we explored how embracing change is crucial to adaptability and flexibility in our dynamic world. Building on that notion, we now turn our focus towards fostering a growth mindset, a fundamental stepping stone towards lifelong learning and personal development.

A growth mindset, a term coined by psychologist Carol Dweck, is the belief that our abilities and intelligence can be developed over time. It's about understanding that our talents are just the starting point, and that dedicated effort can help us soar to new heights. This mindset is instrumental for students and young adults, as it encourages resilience and persistence in the face of challenges.

To develop a growth mindset, it's vital to recognize the power of 'yet.' Whenever confronting something that seems insurmountable, remind yourself that you haven't mastered it yet. This small word signifies that there is a learning curve, and with time and experience, you can overcome initial setbacks. Embrace the journey of becoming rather than solely focusing on immediate accomplishments.

Perseverance is another cornerstone of a growth mindset. View setbacks not as insurmountable obstacles, but as integral parts of the learning process. Each failure is a clear indication of where your understanding needs to grow, which is invaluable in itself. Take Thomas Edison's approach to inventing the light bulb: he found countless ways not to make a light bulb before he discovered one that worked.

Feedback is another crucial element in cultivating a growth mindset. Instead of fearing criticism, see it as a gift. Honest feedback provides specific insights into how you can improve. It's also essential to learn to self-reflect with a critical, yet constructive eye. Evaluate your own progress, identifying areas for growth and celebrating the steps you've taken thus far.

Beyond personal reflection, seek out challenges actively. A growth mindset thrives on challenge and views every difficult task as a chance to grow. When you stretch beyond your comfort zone, you not only learn new skills but also discover personal strengths you might not have been aware of.

Curiosity fuels the growth mindset's engine. Foster a natural desire to learn and understand. When you're genuinely interested in a topic, the process of learning becomes more enjoyable and less a chore. Delve into subjects that fascinate you, and let that passion drive your educational pursuits.

Another practice to encourage a growth mindset is to redefine what it means to be smart. Intelligence isn't just about having all the answers; it's about the willingness to ask questions, to explore, and to engage deeply with learning. Attributing success to learning and effort, rather than innate talent, reinforces the belief that you can improve through hard work.

Collaboration with others can also stimulate a growth mindset. By working with peers, mentors, and teachers, you can gain new perspectives, learn from their experiences, and receive support. Understand that collaborative learning environments are a goldmine for growth, as they allow for the sharing of knowledge and strategies.

Emotional resilience is an integral aspect of developing a growth mindset. It involves handling stress and emotional upheaval in a way that allows you to continue on your path of growth. This means practicing self-compassion, giving yourself permission to be imperfect, and recognizing that growth often comes from discomfort.

Vision setting is another technique to help cultivate a growth mindset. Set clear goals for yourself, both short-term and long-term, to direct your growth. These goals should be specific, measurable, achievable, relevant, and time-bound (SMART), providing you with the roadmap you need to advance.

Along with setting goals, creating a positive affirmation practice can reinforce a growth mindset. Affirmations are positive statements that can help you to challenge and overcome self-sabotaging and negative thoughts. Repeating affirmations can encourage you to maintain an optimistic outlook, even in the face of difficulties.

Consistency is key when nurturing a growth mindset. It's not enough to embrace these principles occasionally; they must become part of your daily routine. Make continuous learning and challenge-seeking behaviors that define your approach to life and personal development.

Finally, remember to be patient with yourself. Developing a growth mindset doesn't happen overnight. It's a gradual process, filled with learning opportunities and moments of both success and failure. Celebrate each step forward, knowing that with each stride, you're shaping a more adaptable, flexible, and capable version of yourself.

In conclusion, a growth mindset is an essential element in becoming an adaptable and flexible individual. It empowers you to take control of your learning and growth, ensuring that you're always evolving and reaching new heights. Embrace this mindset wholeheartedly, and watch as the doors of opportunity swing wide open before you.

Chapter 8:
Leadership and Influence

Transitioning from the personal flexibility detailed in the previous chapter, we now step into the realm of *Leadership and Influence*, where the ripple of one's character can extend to inspire change and ignite passion in others. True leadership isn't about having a title or position; it's about cultivating the ability to shape the future through the empowerment of others. At its core, leadership intertwines with influence—the nuanced art of guiding and encouraging others towards shared goals without coercion. In this chapter, we'll unravel the fibers of what makes a leader truly remarkable and explore how to harness the power of positive influence to foster an environment where ideas flourish, goals are achieved, and individuals feel valued and understood. By mastering the subtleties of influence, you can inspire trust and respect, and lead by example. You'll learn that every interaction is an opportunity to lead, whether you're spearheading a team project, mentoring a peer, or standing up for what's right in your community. The leaders of tomorrow are those who are able to see the horizon through the eyes of many, sculpt their vision with the hands of many, and walk the path of achievement with the footsteps of many. Remember, leadership is not confined within the limits of office walls or organizational charts; it is an open sky, and you have the potential to be the wind beneath the wings of progress. The essence of your journey through leadership and influence begins with understanding the power and responsibility that comes with this role, and this chapter aims to equip you with the insights necessary to step into those shoes with confidence and grace.

What Makes a Leader?

Leadership is multi-faceted and awe-inspiring in its complexity. Each leader is as unique as a fingerprint, yet they share common threads that weave together to form the fabric of influence and guidance. You may find yourself asking, "What truly makes a leader stand out?"

At the core, leadership is not about titles or hierarchies; it's not confined to the corner office or the glimmering badge of a C-suite executive. Instead, it's about the ability to rally people towards a common goal, to light the fire of passion and commitment in others, and to forge a path that others want to follow.

An essential attribute of effective leadership is *vision*. A leader must see beyond the horizon, crafting a clear and compelling picture of the future that ignites excitement and hope. This vision acts as a north star, a guiding light that provides direction and purpose for the team.

But vision alone isn't enough. A true leader possesses the *empathy* to connect with their team on a human level. This emotional intelligence allows a leader to listen deeply, understand nuances, and respond to the needs and aspirations of those they lead. It's the glue that binds a leader's vision to the team's collective heart.

Integrity is another cornerstone of leadership. This is the leader's inner compass, ensuring they stay true to their values and principles regardless of the circumstances. An unwavering commitment to doing what is right builds trust and respect, hallmark traits of any influential leader.

Leaders are often defined by their *decisiveness*. In a world swirling with uncertainties, a leader must make tough choices, sometimes with incomplete information. The courage to make decisions and the resolve to stand by them, while being open to adjust as needed, is a delicate but necessary balancing act.

Another defining quality is *adaptability*, the capacity to pivot in response to change. Leaders are not daunted by shifts in the landscape; rather, they view change as an opportunity for growth and innovation.

Leaders also exhibit *humility*. They recognize that their success rests not on their shoulders alone but on the collaborative efforts of their team. They are quick to distribute credit and just as quick to shoulder responsibility for setbacks.

A leader is a *communicator* par excellence. They articulate ideas clearly and inspire others with their words. More than that, they are outstanding listeners, always seeking to understand before seeking to be understood.

Leaders are builders—of people, teams, and cultures. They *nurture* the potential in others, providing guidance, encouragement, and recognition. They invest in their people, knowing that the strength of their leadership is reflected in the success of those they lead.

The fabric of leader is also woven with *resilience*. They confront challenges head-on and are not easily discouraged. Setbacks are seen as temporary; what matters is the comeback, not the setback.

Leaders are champions of *innovation*. They foster an environment where new ideas are born and tested. They challenge the status quo and push boundaries to find better ways to achieve goals.

An often underappreciated skill of leaders is *patience*. The growth of individuals and the progress toward a vision takes time. Leaders understand this and show persistence and endurance on the journey to success.

Lastly, an extraordinary leader has an infectious *enthusiasm*. Their energy and passion are palpable, and it acts as a catalyst that propels the entire team forward with a shared drive to achieve greatness.

The essence of leadership, therefore, is a rich tapestry of skills, attitudes, and behaviors that together create an individual capable of influencing, guiding, and inspiring others. It's about making a positive impact that resonates beyond the confines of an organization into the broader spectrum of society.

As we delve deeper into leadership and the way it molds our path through life, it becomes evident that the journey of becoming a leader is ever-evolving. It's not a fixed state but a continual process of growth, learning, adaptation, and above all, a commitment to excellence and service.

Leadership is not a mantle that one simply puts on; it is a challenge to rise up to, a mission to fulfill with every fiber of our being. And in this journey of transformation, we uncover the best in ourselves and ignite the potential in others. That is the true essence of leadership. That's what makes a leader.

Techniques for Positive Influence

Building on the pillars of leadership, one must embrace the art of positive influence to truly inspire and guide others toward success. Influencing with positivity isn't about manipulation or sheer exercise of power; it's about creating an environment where others feel valued, understood, and motivated to perform at their best. Here we delve into the techniques that foster such positive influence and galvanize individuals and teams alike.

Firstly, *leading by example* stands as the cornerstone of positive influence. As a leader, your actions speak far louder than words ever could. Demonstrate the work ethic, integrity, and commitment you expect to see in those around you. When team members see these values in action, they are more likely to mirror them, setting a powerful standard for the entire organization.

Another critical technique is *effective communication*. It's not only about conveying your message but also about inviting an open dialogue. Encourage others to share their thoughts and ideas, and truly listen when they do. Acknowledging and incorporating their contributions fosters a sense of ownership and investment in the team's goals.

Emotional intelligence plays a pivotal role in positive influence. The ability to empathize with others, understand their emotions, and respond appropriately can create strong connections and trust. Empathy allows you to navigate sensitive situations with care and encourages a supportive team culture.

Recognition and appreciation go a long way in influencing others positively. Regularly acknowledging individuals' efforts and achievements, both big and small, can boost morale and motivation. This recognition should be genuine and specific, highlighting exactly what actions you value and wish to see continued.

Mentorship and coaching are active forms of influence that can dramatically impact an individual's personal and professional growth. By investing time in developing others' skills and offering guidance, you enable them to reach their potential and show that their success matters to you.

Clear vision and goal setting are also instrumental. When you articulate a compelling vision and break it down into achievable goals, you provide direction and purpose. This clarity helps individuals understand their role in the bigger picture and how their efforts contribute to the collective success.

Flexibility as a leader can also positively influence your team. Demonstrating adaptability in the face of change shows resilience and a forward-thinking mindset. It reassures your team that you can navigate challenges together, no matter what comes your way.

Creating a culture of accountability is another influential technique. When team members know that their commitments carry weight and they are responsible for outcomes, it promotes a sense of responsibility and professionalism. This should be a shared culture, where accountability is not just top-down but a collective commitment.

Modeling a positive attitude, especially during difficult times, sets an emotional tone for the group. A positive outlook can be contagious, helping to keep morale high and encouraging team members to look for solutions rather than dwelling on problems.

Empowering others is also a key technique for positive influence. When you delegate meaningful tasks and decision-making power, it shows trust in your team members' abilities and judgment. Empowerment can lead to innovation and a deeper commitment to shared goals.

Openness to feedback is essential. Encourage and value feedback from all levels of the organization. This openness not only helps you improve as a leader but also demonstrates a genuine interest in continuous learning and development, a mindset that can spread throughout the team.

Consistency in behavior and expectations sets a reliable precedent for what is valued and what is not. It removes uncertainty and enables team members to feel secure in their environments to take calculated risks and be creative within known boundaries.

Finally, fostering a spirit of collaboration rather than competition among team members ensures that the focus remains on collective goals. When the success of one is seen as the success of all, a powerful synergy is created that can overcome even the most challenging obstacles.

In conclusion, positive influence in leadership is about much more than simply getting others to follow your lead. It's about inspiring, encouraging, and empowering them to do their best – not only for the team or organization but for themselves. It's about creating a legacy of leaders who, in turn, will positively influence the world around them.

As we move forward in this journey through the soft skills landscape, remember that your ability to positively influence others can be one of the most transformative aspects of your leadership toolkit. It strengthens all the soft skills you're developing, including negotiation, conflict resolution, and networking, which we'll explore in the chapters ahead. So let's carry these techniques with us as we continue to build our legacy of leadership.

Chapter 9:
Negotiation and Conflict Resolution

In the grand tapestry of soft skills, the threads of negotiation and conflict resolution are pivotal in weaving a pattern of success. Life continuously presents a myriad of scenarios requiring us to negotiate and resolve conflicts, whether it's finalizing a project deadline or navigating the complexities of human relationships. Mastering these skills isn't just about reaching agreeable outcomes; it's about creating value in our interactions and fostering sustainable relationships. Imagine the art of negotiation as a dance, where empathy and strategy move in harmony to the rhythm of mutual respect. Likewise, resolving conflict is akin to being a sculptor; it involves chiseling away at misunderstandings to reveal the masterpiece of common ground beneath. Every encounter is a platform to practice, every conversation a chance to refine your approach, and every disagreement an opportunity to enhance your skill at turning adversity into progress. Embrace these skills with the understanding that their mastery can become one of your greatest assets, empowering you to navigate life's challenges with confidence and poise.

The Art of Negotiation

It's a transformative moment when you come to the realization that negotiation is not just a skill, but an art, one that calls for creativity, intuition, and an understanding of human nature. In this journey through the realms of negotiation, we'll explore how this art form weaves itself into the tapestry of successful interactions and outcomes.

Firstly, it's imperative to grasp that negotiation isn't about winning or losing. It's about finding a harmony between parties where both feel they have gained value. The mindset with which you approach a negotiation sets the tone. See the individual across the table not as an adversary, but as a partner in problem-solving. This frame of mind paves the way to solutions that are fruitful for all involved.

Preparation is the foundation of negotiation. Before you enter discussions, research thoroughly. Understand the context, the needs, the wants, and the limitations of both your own position and that of the other party. Knowledge isn't just power; it's the compass that guides you through the negotiation landscape, allowing you to navigate with confidence and strategic foresight.

Effective communication stands at the core of negotiation. You've learned about the significance of verbal and non-verbal cues already. In the negotiation arena, how you convey your propositions and how actively you listen are pivotal. Your words should be clear and your objectives succinct, while your capacity to listen will help you perceive what is—and isn't—being said, enabling you to address any undercurrents at play.

Then there's emotional intelligence, a cornerstone in the architecture of negotiation. Being attuned to the emotional atmosphere can give you a significant advantage. It's about empathy, understanding the emotions of the other person, and managing your own. An emotionally intelligent negotiator can defuse tension and foster an environment where openness and collaboration can thrive.

Yet, even with emotional intelligence, communication skills, and preparation, the unpredictable nature of human interactions can turn the tide of any negotiation. Here's where adaptability comes into play.

Sometimes, the road to agreement means taking unexpected detours. Stay flexible, without losing sight of your goals, and you can maneuver through twists and turns that might thwart the less adaptable negotiator.

Now, let's not forget the power of asking the right questions. Questions are the keys that unlock hidden interests and motivations. They demonstrate your engagement and may reveal insights that could be pivotal in reaching an agreement that meets both parties' core interests.

Alongside questions, active listening solidifies your understanding of the other party's stance. Reflecting on what they say and clarifying points not only enhances your comprehension but also shows respect. This can help build rapport, a golden bridge leading towards a mutually acceptable solution.

Negotiation is inherently strategic, and knowing when and how to make concessions is a delicate dance. Your concessions should be purposeful, trading what is of lesser importance to you for what you value more highly. All the while, understanding the other party's concessions fortifies the strategic positioning of your requests.

Deadlocks can occur, no matter how skilled the negotiator. A deadlock, however, doesn't spell the end. Instead, it's an opportunity to showcase creativity and innovation. Maybe it's time to introduce new ideas or reframe the situation. A breakthrough often lies just beyond the impasse, waiting for the innovative thinker to uncover it.

Patience is a virtue often underscored in successful negotiations. The eagerness to rush to an agreement can undermine the quality of the deal you strike. Time can be a strategic ally, allowing for more thoughtful consideration and for each side to envision the benefits of an agreement.

Throughout your negotiations, maintain integrity and transparency. A reputation for honesty establishes trust, an invaluable currency in the exchange of negotiation. And while it's important to be assertive in representing your interests, balancing this with respect and consideration for the other party's needs fortifies long-term relationships, paving the way for future interactions.

Closing a negotiation is as much art as beginning one. Summarize the key points, restate the value of the agreement to both parties, and capture the terms in writing. A well-crafted agreement is the seal on a successful negotiation, formalizing the understanding and setting the stage for successful implementation.

As we conclude this discussion on the art of negotiation, remember that it's a skill that can always be honed. Each interaction you have is an opportunity to practice and refine your approach. Be deliberate in your negotiations, attentive to the process, and reflective after each experience. It's through continuous learning and practice that mastery is achieved.

Negotiation, at its finest, is about creating possibilities, expanding the pie rather than fighting over the slices. With each successful negotiation, you don't just reach an agreement; you build a bridge, foster understanding, and, quite possibly, shape a shared future. As you practice this art, may you find in yourself not just adeptness, but a sense of fulfillment and a recognition of your growth in this most human of arts.

Strategies for Conflict Resolution

In the preceding sections, we explored the nuanced landscape of negotiation. But what happens when negotiations take a sharp turn into conflict territory? Conflict is an inevitable part of life. Whether you're navigating a misunderstanding with a classmate or facing a standoff with a colleague, mastering conflict resolution is crucial. So let's embark on a journey to transform discord into harmony.

Firstly, it's essential to understand that conflict isn't inherently negative. It can lead to growth, innovation, and stronger relationships if handled with care and skill. Embracing conflict as an opportunity rather than a threat sets the stage for constructive resolution. This mindset shift is a foundational step in managing disagreements effectively.

One powerful strategy is to practice active listening. When tensions rise, we often succumb to the urge to defend our position without fully comprehending the other party's perspective. Intentional listening involves paying close attention, asking clarifying questions, and repeating back what you've heard, ensuring you both understand and are understood.

Consider also the art of empathy. Placing yourself in another's shoes can be transformative. It's about more than seeing their point of view but genuinely feeling it. Empathy doesn't mean you have to agree, but it facilitates a respectful dialogue where solutions can surface from mutual understanding.

Effective communication is the bridge that connects conflicting sides. Clarity, honesty, and respect should be the pillars of your conversations. Use "I" statements to express your feelings without blaming or attacking, which can lead to defensiveness and escalate the conflict.

Fostering a collaborative environment is also instrumental for conflict resolution. When both parties commit to finding a mutually beneficial solution, the process shifts from adversarial to cooperative. It's not about winning or losing; it's about emerging from the conflict with a win-win outcome.

Sometimes, the best approach is to take a timeout. In the heat of conflict, emotions can cloud judgment. Stepping away to cool down can provide the clarity needed to revisit the situation with a level head. Use this time to reflect, not ruminate, preparing yourself to return to the discussion with a renewed focus on resolution.

Developing your ability to articulate complex ideas simply and respectfully is another crucial aspect of resolving conflicts. Complexity can beget confusion, fueling conflict. Strive for simplicity in your communication, as it can lead to more effective and quicker resolutions.

Creating a roadmap for resolution can provide a concrete path to follow during conflict. This could involve setting ground rules for engagement or developing a step-by-step plan to address each issue. A structured approach provides a sense of security and clarity for all involved.

Don't underestimate the role of negotiating skills in conflict resolution. Effective negotiating enables you to make concessions that cost you little but mean a lot to the other person. Understanding the art of compromise ensures that you leave no stone unturned in your quest for peace.

Another facet to consider is the importance of cultural sensitivity. In our diverse world, conflicts sometimes arise from cultural misunderstandings. Demonstrating respect for cultural differences and being willing to learn can go a long way toward peaceful resolutions.

When conflicts seem unresolvable, it might be time to bring in a third party. A neutral mediator can offer fresh perspectives and facilitate dialogue that leads to a breakthrough. It's not a sign of weakness to seek help; rather, it's a commitment to resolution.

It's also valuable to look beyond the immediate conflict and see the bigger picture. How will the resolution of this conflict serve your long-term goals and relationships? Keeping the future in mind can provide the motivation to resolve conflicts in a way that supports your journey.

Remember, the goal of conflict resolution isn't to emerge victorious but to arrive at a solution that respects the needs and wants of everyone. It's a delicate dance of give and take, backed by a desire to maintain and strengthen relationships.

Lastly, view each conflict as a learning experience. After the dust has settled, reflect on what worked, what didn't, and how you can improve your conflict resolution skills moving forward. This reflective practice will arm you with wisdom for the inevitable future disputes.

Embrace these strategies with an open heart and a willing mind, and you'll find that resolving conflicts becomes less daunting and more a part of the natural ebb and flow of human interaction. As we move forward, remember that the ability to navigate the complex world of human emotions and interactions is a powerful tool at your disposal for crafting a successful and harmonious life path.

Chapter 10:
Time Management and Productivity

As we continue to unravel the tapestry of soft skills essential for success, let's delve into the heart of efficiency—time management and productivity. These are not mere concepts, but the very engine that drives our ability to achieve goals, fulfill our potential, and savor life's moments. Imagine equipping yourself with the skill to transform the relentless ticking of the clock into a rhythm that dances to your own beat. It's about gaining an intimate understanding of your priorities and using that knowledge to navigate through life's demands with grace. With the right strategies, tools, and mindset, you can elevate your productivity, not by racing against time, but by harmoniously syncing your actions with your aspirations. This chapter isn't just about getting more done in less time; it's about making each moment count, ensuring that what you're doing aligns with your broader vision. By mastering time management, you'll not only propel yourself towards your goals, but you'll also cultivate a life rich in purpose and devoid of unnecessary stress. Approach each day as an opportunity, embrace the tools that create order out of chaos, and watch as the pieces of your puzzle fall seamlessly into place.

Setting Priorities and Goals

In the ongoing journey toward self-improvement and success, understanding how to effectively manage your time through setting priorities and goals is not just a skill - it's an essential compass for navigating the complex waters of daily life. As we delve into this crucial aspect of time management and productivity, remember that the foundation of achieving anything of value rests upon clear, actionable objectives and the ability to discern what's most important.

Establishing priorities begins with recognizing that not all tasks and goals are created equal. A scattered focus leads to mediocre results, while a laser-like attention on the right priorities propels you forward incredibly. Think of setting priorities as laying down the groundwork for a building—without a solid foundation, the structure can't stand tall. Identifying these priorities means asking yourself which activities contribute the most value to your academic pursuits, personal growth, and future aspirations.

Goal setting, on the other hand, is the blueprints for your foundation. Goals provide a clear endpoint to your efforts, making it easier to map out the path to success. When crafting goals, it's important to ensure they are SMART: Specific, Measurable, Achievable, Relevant, and Time-bound. This framework transforms nebulous dreams into achievable targets, rendering the once daunting journey into a series of manageable steps.

As you're setting these goals, remember to align them with your core values and long-term vision. This alignment will not only spur motivation but will also keep you anchored during times of difficulty or distraction. Your goals should excite you, stir your passion, and feel like a natural extension of your deepest desires and interests.

Visualize the outcome of reaching your goals. Visualization isn't just a buzzword; it's a powerful tool that can galvanize your subconscious into action. By vividly picturing your success, you cement the endgame in your mind's eye, which in turn reinforces your commitment to the process required to get there.

Balancing your priorities is also a dance of understanding the difference between urgent and important. Urgent tasks demand immediate attention but are often tied to someone else's goals. Important tasks, however, are the ones that contribute to your long-term mission, values, and goals. Learning to prioritize the important over the urgent is a skill that can tremendously enhance your productivity and focus.

Time management is fundamentally about saying no to things that are low on your priority list so that you can say yes to those that are high on it. Learning to say no, to turn down invites, requests, and distractions that do not align with your goals, is a skill unto itself. This doesn't mean you become inconsiderate, but rather that you become a guardian of your most precious resource: time.

When setting your priorities and goals, it's crucial to conduct a regular review. This isn't meant to be a grueling self-audit but an honest reflection session to keep your efforts aligned with your objectives. It's a checkpoint to assess progress, recalibrate strategies, and recommit to your goals. What seemed important a month ago may no longer hold the same weight today.

Embrace the mentality of continuous improvement. The pursuit of excellence is never static, and your goals should stretch you slightly beyond your current capabilities. Each goal met should be a stepping stone to a higher, yet attainable, aim. This progressive advancement ensures that your journey is marked with personal growth and meaningful achievement.

Do not underestimate the power of writing down your goals and priorities. The physical act of writing not only helps you to remember but also to clarify your thoughts. Having them in a tangible form also allows you to revisit and revise them as you grow and as circumstances evolve.

Practice patience and perseverance. The road to accomplishing your goals is often long and winding, with its fair share of setbacks. When you face obstacles, view them as tests of your resolve and opportunities for learning and refinement, not as stop signs.

Finally, prioritize balance in your life. Goals and priorities shouldn't chain you to a desk or a single pursuit; they should also include personal development, relationships, health, and leisure. A well-rounded life supports a sustainable pace and prevents burnout, ensuring that you remain productive and engaged over the long term.

Remember, time is the canvas on which you paint the masterpiece of your life. By setting priorities and goals, you determine the image that ultimately emerges. This process isn't about being rigid and unyielding; it's about steering your ship with intention and precision, even when storms arise and the seas are unpredictable.

Cultivating the art of setting priorities and goals isn't just about achieving more; it's about achieving what truly matters. As you continue on your journey, bolstered by the soft skills you're acquiring, you will find that this particular competence serves not only as a cornerstone of time management but as an essential element of an impactful, fruitful, and fulfilling life.

Tools and Techniques for Time Management

Effective time management is the keystone of productivity. It's the ability to organize and plan how much time you spend on specific activities, which, in turn, can lead to greater success in your academic, personal, and professional life. But how do you harness this powerful skill? Let's explore the tools and techniques that can help you manage time wisely.

First and foremost, **goal setting** is at the heart of time management. Take time to define what you want to achieve — your goals should be SMART: Specific, Measurable, Achievable, Relevant, and Timely. Clear goals give you a destination and a roadmap to get there, ensuring that you're not wandering aimlessly.

To-do lists are a classic tool but remain incredibly effective. They provide a visual reminder of tasks and can be satisfying to update as you complete each item. Keep your list organized and prioritize tasks by deadline and importance. Over time, you'll get a sense of accomplishment seeing the checked items grow, and it'll inspire you to keep the momentum.

Calendars and planners are indispensable for managing your daily, weekly, and monthly agendas. Digital calendars can be particularly useful, allowing you to set reminders, alerts, and even share schedules with others. And don't underestimate the power of a traditional paper planner – the act of writing things down can reinforce your memory of them.

Adopt **time blocking** as a way to allocate specific hours to particular tasks or types of work. This is like setting an appointment with yourself to focus on a task without interruptions. It creates structure in your day and can dramatically increase your productivity by keeping you focused on one task at a time.

Now, consider the **Pomodoro Technique**, a time management method that breaks down work into intervals, traditionally 25 minutes in length. This technique is effective because it creates urgency and a sense of a ticking clock, which can help sharpen your focus.

Another essential tool is **task delegation**. Recognize tasks that others can do for you or with you. It's not just a way to share the load but also an opportunity to empower others—a win-win for time management and collaboration.

Time tracking apps can provide insight into exactly where your time is going. By monitoring the time you spend on tasks, you can identify areas where you're spending too much or too little time and adjust accordingly.

Minimize interruptions by using tools like **website blockers** and notifications silencers during work sessions. These interruptions can fragment your time and attention, making it hard to regain focus. Protecting your time is an active step towards better productivity.

Invest time in **learning and education**. Though it may seem counterintuitive to spend time to save time, learning new skills or software that can automate or speed up your work is a valuable investment. This also includes honing your own skills in time management.

Personalize your approach to time management – what works for someone else may not work for you. Through trial and error, discover the techniques that best align with your workflow and lifestyle. Adaptability is key to finding what genuinely enhances your productivity.

The most important aspect of all these tools and techniques is consistency. Make time management a regular part of your routine. The more you practice, the more natural it will become, and you'll start to see the benefits spill over into all areas of your life.

Remember to schedule breaks and downtime as well. Time management is not just about working smarter but also about ensuring that you have time to recharge and maintain your mental health. Balance is crucial — without it, burnout looms.

Moreover, don't get discouraged if things don't go as planned. Time management is a skill that improves with persistence. Even small improvements can make a significant impact on your productivity and well-being.

Finally, reflect regularly on how you're spending your time. Are your actions aligning with your priorities and goals? Self-reflection not only refines your time management skills but also keeps you true to your journey toward success in all your endeavors.

The mastery of time management opens up a world of productivity, where deadlines are met with confidence and goals are achieved with precision. Embrace these tools and techniques, and you will unlock the potential to create a life that is well-organized, less stressful, and rich in accomplishments. It's about finding harmony in the hustle, ensuring that every minute is not just spent, but invested wisely towards building the future you aspire to.

Chapter 11:
Networking and Relationship Building

As we transition from the structured rigor of time management and leap into the flowing world of human connections, we reach a pivotal chapter that could very well be the heart of professional success: Networking and Relationship Building. The strength of your network is not merely in the numbers you collect, but in the depth of your connections and the mutual value you create through them. Imagine the vast potential of resources, knowledge, and opportunities that are often just a handshake or a conversation away. Here, we emphasize the skilled artistry of forming bonds that go beyond superficial interactions and dive into creating durable, mutually beneficial relationships. It's about nurturing a sense of trust and camaraderie that can catapult careers and enrich lives. Through genuine engagement and the sharing of expertise, the most successful individuals don't just build a network—they foster a community that supports, inspires, and propels each other towards greatness.

The Power of Networking

In the fabric of professional growth, the threads that interconnect us with others are not just nice-to-have adornments; they are the very weft and warp that strengthen the material of our careers. This strength, this potent force that has the power to shape our career path, is networking.

What often goes unspoken in the lexicon of success is that opportunities tend to flow through human connections. Networking isn't merely shaking hands and exchanging business cards—it's about cultivating a circle of influence, a community of support that will open doors and bring those opportunities to light. It is about building bridges before you need to cross them.

Let's reflect on an indisputable fact: we live in an interconnected world where the proverbial six degrees of separation become even fewer within professional circles. The right connection can mean the difference between a missed chance and a pivotal career move. Networking weaves a safety net so that when you take those leaps of faith in your career, there's something—or someone—to catch you.

Networking is reciprocal by nature. It is not hoarding contacts, but rather creating and sharing value. Engaging with others in your industry isn't a one-way street. Think not only of what your network can do for you, but also of how you can add value to your network. Can you offer insight, resources, or introductions? The adage 'It's not what you know, but who you know' lacks nuance; it's actually about who knows you and what they know you for.

Indeed, the richest resource one can have is a diverse network of individuals. Diversity in networking means creating connections with people from different industries, backgrounds, and expertise areas. It boosts innovation, as fresh perspectives challenge the status quo. It encourages personal growth, as varying viewpoints broaden one's horizon. Simply put, a diverse network is a vast expanse of potential and possibilities.

Keep in mind, the foundation of solid networking is built on sincerity and authenticity. People can sense when someone is trying to use them as a stepping-stone, which can burn bridges rather than build them. Authentic engagement with others is about being true to yourself and genuinely interested in those you meet. It's about finding common interests and shared values that fuel long-term relationships.

It is important to remember that networking does not end with making a connection; it thrives on nurturing that connection. Like seeds in a garden, professional relationships require care and attention to grow. Regular check-ins, sharing information of mutual interest, or even a simple 'how are you?' keeps the relationship alive and meaningful.

Professional networking today has expanded beyond the confines of local business mixers and industry events. Platforms such as LinkedIn enable us to network globally, allowing us to reach out and connect with professionals from all around the world. But with great power comes great responsibility; your digital presence must mirror the professionalism and integrity you showcase in person.

Becoming proficient at networking also involves mastering the art of small talk. Engaging in light conversation breaks the ice and lays the groundwork for a deeper dialogue. By showing genuine interest in another person's views, experiences, and challenges, we not only garner information but also build rapport and trust.

Moreover, successful networking strategies recognize that timing is everything. Sensitivity to when you approach someone and how you follow up can reflect your professionalism. Whether you're reaching out after a conference or reminding someone of a chance encounter, the manner and timing of your communication often dictate its success.

Let us not ignore the role of mentorship within the networking sphere. A mentor, often found through initial networking efforts, can accelerate your professional development. They can guide you, provide advice, and importantly, introduce you to their networks, further expanding your circle of influence.

Networking also requires a certain level of courage. Walking into a room full of strangers and introducing yourself can be daunting. But remember, courage is not the absence of fear; it's the judgment that something else is more important than fear. In networking, the belief in the value of making new connections conquers the temporary discomfort of reaching out.

Furthermore, the best networkers are also active listeners. Much more than waiting for your turn to speak, active listening means being fully present in the conversation, absorbing and responding thoughtfully to what others are saying. This not only garners respect but also ensures that the conversation will be remembered as meaningful by all participants.

The potential of networking is not to be underestimated. When done correctly, it fosters an ecosystem that can cultivate innovation, mentorship, and career growth. It enables you to tap into a wealth of knowledge and opportunities that lie within the collective reach of those you are connected to. So, as you move forward, let the power of networking be the guide by which you navigate the complex waters of your professional journey.

As this section seamlessly weaves into the next, know that networking is more than just forming connections; it's about crafting relationships that endure and evolve. The next chapter will delve deeper into creating and maintaining these meaningful relationships—not just for the sake of a rolodex brimming with contacts but for developing a community that emboldens both professional and personal growth.

Creating and Maintaining Meaningful Relationships

As we delve into the core of networking, let's illuminate the path to forging not just connections, but meaningful relationships.

Relationships are the bridge to personal and professional success, not just a mere ornament to your career landscape. It's about knitting a pattern of bonds that hold not only shared interests but shared values, trust, and mutual respect as well.

Embarking on this journey, remember that relationships aren't built overnight. It's a gradual process that flourishes with time and genuine interactions. Think of them as seeds that, when nurtured with sincerity and consistent effort, blossom into a garden of alliances that can weather the most formidable storms.

The cornerstone of building a meaningful relationship is authenticity. Be genuine in your approach. People can sense when someone is not being their true self, and it sets off alarms. Your genuine interest in another person's story, challenges, and successes paves the way for a deeper connection. Be yourself, because originality never goes out of style.

Listening is just as critical as sharing. Active listening demonstrates that you value the other person's words and their perspective. It's a powerful way to show respect and form a bond grounded in understanding. When we listen with the intent to comprehend, rather than simply to reply, we make conversations more meaningful and relationships stronger.

Consistency is another key element; it's the rhythm that keeps the melody of the relationship playing. Stay in touch, be responsive and make sure your actions mirror the promises you've made. Small gestures, like remembering and acknowledging special moments in their lives, can have a huge impact and propel your relationship forward.

To maintain these relationships, the focus must shift from taking to giving. Ask yourself, "What can I contribute to this relationship?" The most enduring relationships are those where both parties feel they are receiving and contributing value. Be that person who isn't just there in triumphant moments, but also when the chips are down.

Flexibility and openness to diverse perspectives strengthen relationships. Understand that disagreements are part of any relationship, but they don't have to lead to its demise. Embrace differences as a way to expand your own horizons and strengthen the connection.

Building trust is paramount, and it's something you can't rush. Trust is earned through consistent actions over time. Be reliable and maintain confidentiality. When people know they can rely on you, they're more likely to reciprocate trust and invest in the relationship.

Personalization goes a long way; treat each relationship uniquely. Understand what motivates the other person, their likes, dislikes, and personal aspirations. Tailored gestures and communication can resonate more profoundly than generic ones.

Let's not forget the power of positivity. Positive energy is contagious and can transform the atmosphere and dynamic of your interactions. Maintaining an optimistic outlook can inspire not only you but also those around you to invest more deeply in the relationship.

Virtual connections have their place, but nothing replaces the impact of face-to-face interactions. Make the effort to meet in person whenever possible. The shared experiences and memories created in person are invaluable to relationship-building.

Never underestimate the power of a simple 'thank you.' Expressing gratitude shows appreciation for the other person's presence in your life, and it can reinforce the strength of your bond. A heartfelt acknowledgment of someone's help or support is the kind of currency that never deflates in value.

As you grow and evolve, allow your relationships to do the same. People change, and so do their circumstances, needs, and abilities to contribute. Keeping pace with these changes—and embracing them—can keep relationships vibrant and dynamic.

Finally, understand that not all relationships are meant to last a lifetime. Some serve a purpose for a specific time or season, and when that period ends, it's okay to let go with grace. Cherish the value they've added to your life, and move forward with the lessons they've taught you.

In sum, creating and maintaining meaningful relationships is akin to artistry. It requires passion, patience, and persistence. Each relationship is a masterpiece that you co-create, adding depth and enrichment to the tapestry of your life. So, invest your heart and mind in these bonds, for they can be the strongest support systems in your journey towards success and fulfillment.

Chapter 12:
Professionalism and Work Ethic

As we delve into the heart of what sets a truly remarkable professional apart, you'll discover that your presence, punctuality, preparation, poise, and politeness are much more than mere alliteration; they are the pillars that distinguish an individual in the workplace. Professionalism isn't just about wearing the right attire or uttering the correct jargon; it's an internalized ethos that radiates integrity and responsibility. Upholding a stalwart work ethic means consistently exceeding expectations, being reliable, and taking initiative—it's about cultivating a reputation of excellence. This chapter isn't merely about adhering to a code of conduct; it's an invitation to embody the quality that can transform an occupation into an art form. By weaving professionalism and a steadfast work ethic into your being, you'll not only elevate your career but will also set a standard that inspires those around you to strive for greatness.

The Importance of Professionalism

Ascending the ladder of success isn't merely about mastering technical know-how; it's about ingraining professionalism into every fiber of your being. Professionalism is the cement that fortifies the foundation of your career and casts you in the most favorable light possible in any vocational setting.

In essence, professionalism is an amalgamation of several key soft skills—those integral attributes that enable us to navigate the world, collaborate with others, and pursue our goals with tenacity. It's the polish on the shoe, the firm handshake, and the attentive gaze during a conversation. It encapsulates not just what you do, but how you do it.

Consider professionalism as your personal brand—a representation of your commitment to excellence, regardless of the task at hand. More than just genteel manners, it's a commitment to ethical behavior, reliability, and respect for others. This dimension of your work persona informs the world you're serious about contributing something worthwhile, and that your word is both your bond and your badge of honor.

Professionalism sets the high-flyers apart from the crowd. It whispers of competence and speaks volumes about your ability to lead, to be trusted, and to be held accountable. This is why employers place such a premium on this trait. They're not just hiring a set of skills; they're hiring a whole person—a professional.

But why should professionalism carry such weight? The workplace is a mosaic of personalities, a cross-section of society where different values, attitudes, and behaviors converge. Professionalism is the glue that holds these pieces together, creating a cohesive, productive space. Without this key element, the work environment risks falling into discord and inefficiency.

Let's delve deeper into the intertwining facets of professionalism. Firstly, it involves effective communication. Miscommunication can be a major hindrance to progress, but a professional knows how to convey ideas clearly and listen attentively, fostering mutual understanding and respect.

Aligned with communication is emotional intelligence—the ability to empathize, control one's emotions, and read the room. A professional person knows that emotional outbursts or indifference can strain work relationships and disrupt the workflow.

Another cornerstone of professionalism is timekeeping. It's about valuing not just your time but that of your colleagues and clients. Being punctual for meetings and deadlines speaks to your reliability and respect for others, while lateness can tarnish your reputation.

Moreover, professionalism embraces the spirit of teamwork and collaboration. It's knowing that the sum is indeed greater than its parts and that being a supportive team player leads to collective triumphs. A professional stays open to others' ideas and recognizes that diverse perspectives can yield game-changing solutions.

It also involves a dedication to continuous learning and growth. A professional knows that the world doesn't stand still and that staying abreast of industry trends and expanding one's expertise are paramount. This eagerness to learn radiates a certain drive and ambition that is infectious.

But perhaps the most defining attribute of a professional is integrity. It's about doing the right thing, even when no one is watching. Integrity builds trust, and trust breeds opportunities. Professionalism without integrity is like a lamp without light—it lacks its fundamental purpose.

Professionalism is also reflected in one's appearance and behavior. They say clothes make the man—or woman—and in the world of work, how you present yourself can either enhance or detract from your professional image.

Lastly, a robust work ethic is an intractable part of professionalism. It's about showing up, not just physically, but mentally, emotionally, and with a passion that turns tasks into achievements and jobs into careers. It's the unwavering commitment to not just meet but exceed expectations.

The workplace will challenge you, and how you respond to these challenges marks your level of professionalism. It's in the difficulties that your professionalism is not only tested but also recognized and remembered. You become a beacon for others to follow—a role model in a world that values the blend of soft skills that constitute professionalism.

Inculcating professionalism into your personal doctrine demands effort, reflection, and a willingness to adapt. It's a continuous journey rather than a destination. As you journey through your career, remember that professionalism is an investment with immeasurable returns. It opens doors, builds bridges, and paves the road to both personal and professional fulfillment.

So embrace it. Nurture it. Let it become so ingrained in who you are that it shines effortlessly through your work and interactions. In this way, your professional journey won't just lead to success—it will be marked by a legacy of respect, excellence, and integrity.

Cultivating a Strong Work Ethic

As we delve into the backbone of career success, we land squarely on the bedrock of professionalism: a robust work ethic. It's the quiet engine in most success stories, a consistent thread woven into the fabric of accomplished careers. A strong work ethic is less about the number of hours spent toiling away and more about the quality, consistency, and vigor you bring to those hours. It's a creed that guides professionals to do right by their work, even when no one's watching.

Building a strong work ethic requires a blend of motivation, dedication, and a sense of responsibility. This means rising to meet the demands of your tasks, irrespective of their appeal. It's about showing up, not merely physically, but mentally, with the full force of your concentration and capabilities. A strong work ethic is founded on the belief that the work you do matters, and so, you must give it your very best. Every single day, remind yourself why you chose this path - let the purpose fuel your commitment.

At the core of this tenacity sits self-discipline, a pivotal skill in setting and stomaching the hard boundaries needed to succeed. Anyone can be ordinary, but it takes discipline to chart a course toward extraordinary. Wake up a little earlier, plan your day, and hold yourself accountable for the tasks you set. Every small act of discipline solidifies the compound interest of your work ethic. Remember, in this colossal world, discipline sets champions apart.

Consistency is another cornerstone. You can't just flash a streak of brilliance and then wane into mediocrity. A strong work ethic is about being a reliable beacon of performance, day in and day out. Make your output so consistent that when anomalies occur, they're regarded as outliers, not the norm. Your consistency establishes your reputation, and trust me, your professional reputation precedes you in rooms you've not yet entered.

Stay proactive in your endeavors—don't wait to be told what to do. If you can anticipate a need and address it first, you've just multiplied your value. Being proactive is like setting the dominoes up in such astute alignment that when opportunity nudges the first one, the rest falls into a triumphant cascade showcasing your foresight and initiative.

Quality work is the flagbearer of a strong work ethic. There's an indelible pride that comes from knowing you've given a task everything you had, creating something that stands up to scrutiny and surpasses expectations. Strive for excellence, not perfection. Excellence is attainable, sustainable and places you on a pedestal of reliability and pride in your own contributions.

Adopt a learner's mindset, as continuous improvement is the lifeline of a vigorous work ethic. When you're committed to learning, growth naturally follows. No skill is beneath you, and every encounter is an opportunity to glean something new. Look at challenges as puzzles to solve, not burdens to bear. Shift your focus from problems to solutions, from roadblocks to learning opportunitie

Remember, resilience is a massively undervalued component of work ethic. It's not just about working when the sun shines but also plowing through when storms hit. Successful individuals aren't those who never fail but those who never quit. When faced with setbacks, dust off, learn the lessons, and forge ahead with newfound wisdom. Resilience means being stubborn about your goals but flexible in your methods.

Communication is pivotal even when discussing work ethic. Articulating your thoughts, listening actively, and receiving feedback graciously are all integral to refining the quality of your work. Moreover, clear communication fosters team dynamics where your strong work ethic can influence others, exponentially amplifying productivity.

Gratitude, surprisingly, also ties into work ethic. Be thankful for your opportunities, and recognize the efforts of those around you. Appreciation is a form of emotional generosity that pays dividends in motivation and workplace morale. Never underestimate the power of a simple 'thank you' for a job well done, especially when you're leading others. It can rekindle zeal and dedication like little else.

Time management plays an integral role as well; a strong work ethic is not synonymous with burnout. It's about the smart allocation of your time, ensuring you make the most out of each hour without sacrificing your well-being. Prioritize, delegate as needed, and know when to step back and recharge. Through this, you'll maintain quality and consistency over time without fizzling out.

Don't forget the role of integrity in cultivating a strong work ethic. It's about honesty in your dealings and transparency in your conduct. Your work ethic should fortify an image of you as someone who does the right thing even when it's difficult. Cultivating an environment of trust encourages collective efforts to be geared toward a shared vision of excellence.

Above all, stay humble. No matter how high you rise or how much you achieve, a strong work ethic means remaining grounded. There's always more to learn and room for improvement. Arrogance stifles growth and repels others – be expansive instead. Embrace humility as it's one of the most magnetic qualities in a professional's character.

In conclusion, cultivating a strong work ethic isn't an overnight feat—it's a journey. It's carved out of daily habits, attitude adjustments, and the resolute pursuit of excellence in every action undertaken. Nurture this prized attribute and watch as doors open, opportunities arise, and your story writes itself with the ink of unwavering commitment and zeal for your craft.

As you continue to deepen your proficiency in soft skills, harnessing a robust work ethic will amplify your journey, propelling you towards a rewarding professional life enriched with achievements, respect, and personal fulfillment. Let your work ethic be your silent ambassador, the unseen force that quietly elevates your potential and proclaims your readiness for the greatness that lies ahead.

Chapter 13:
Integrating Soft Skills into Your Life's Journey

Welcome to the culmination of our exploration into the transformative world of soft skills. Throughout this journey, we've unpacked the essence of what makes these abilities so vital in personal and professional realms. By now, you've gained insight into the fabric of communication, the dynamics of emotional intelligence, and the finesse required for effective problem-solving, among others. But the most critical phase is now upon you: the integration of these soft skills into the tapestry of your life.

Think of soft skills as the threads that hold together the fabric of your career and personal growth. They're subtle yet strong, often making the difference between an ordinary and an extraordinary life journey. Each encounter offers an opportunity to weave these skills into your interactions, approach, and the way you handle adversity and success alike.

Consider the importance of adaptability and flexibility, which you've learned are indispensable amid the age-old tides of change. Life is unpredictable, and it's your nimble response to unforeseen events that often shapes the path ahead. Emulating the traits of water — flowing smoothly around obstacles and adapting to the shape of the environment — can guide you through challenging and changing landscapes with grace.

Throughout this book, leadership and influence have been highlighted as keystones in the arch of personal development. These qualities are not just reserved for those in executive suites or positions of authority. You lead by example, you lead with your decisions, and you lead each time you inspire someone to believe in the better they haven't seen in themselves yet.

Effective negotiation and conflict resolution, tools once confined to boardrooms and diplomatic tables, are now recognized as quintessential for maintaining harmony in all areas of life. It's through the respectful exchange of differing views and the forging of mutual understanding that lasting progress is made. Be willing to engage in the dance of give-and-take, allowing you to resolve conflicts with a sense of balance and equity.

Time management and productivity are not about racing against the clock, but rather embracing each moment. It's in being present and focused, acknowledging that while time is a finite resource, your impact within that time is boundless. Prioritize, organize, and execute with a clear vision, all the while understanding that it's okay to pause and breathe.

As you've seen, networking and building relationships transcend professional boundaries. These bridges between human beings enable the sharing of wisdom, support during trials, and collective celebration during triumphs. Cherish these connections, for they are touchstones on your journey—a testament to the shared human experience.

Professionalism and work ethic have been a running theme, emphasizing the value of showing up as your best self. This doesn't just mean in attire or punctuality but in the earnest endeavor to contribute positively to every task and interaction. Your reputation is a mirror of your dedication and integrity.

Let's talk integration. 'How', you might wonder, 'do I take each of these and make them a living, breathing aspect of who I am?' The answer lies in conscious practice and reflection. Commit to observing yourself and your interactions. Are you listening actively? Are you leading empathy in your communication? Are you fostering collaboration with an open heart and mind? This mindfulness is the foundation upon which skillful habits are built.

Take it one step at a time. Select one soft skill you've resonated with most deeply and actively focus on enhancing it. Once you feel confident, move onto another. Remember, it's not about overnight transformation; it's a continual process of layering these skills into the complex, beautiful mosaic of your life's journey.

Rise to the challenge of viewing every day as a learning opportunity. Just as athletes practice to refine their abilities, so too must you exercise your soft skills with persistence. Encountering setbacks is not a signal of failure but a natural and expected element of growth. Failures are the rough grain of sand that creates the pearl; they are part of crafting your expertise in soft skills.

Celebrate your victories, no matter how small. Each successful application of a soft skill is a win to be acknowledged. These moments reaffirm your progress and motivate continual development. Through celebration, you recharge your dedication to lifelong learning and self-improvement.

Remember, integrating soft skills is not a task to be checked off but an ongoing evolution of your character. As you apply these competencies with intention, you'll begin to see a world ripe with new opportunities, relationships, and achievements. They'll become a second nature, guiding you intuitively through the complexities of life.

As you stand poised on the brink of the next chapter, equipped with a trove of invaluable soft skills, remember that the journey you're embarking on is uniquely yours. It's a path decorated with infinite potential, and you've been furnished with the tools to navigate it masterfully.

Embrace each day with the knowledge that these skills are not static; they will evolve and mature with you. As you forge ahead, may the art and science of soft skills be your compass and guide, leading you to horizons filled with fulfillment and unparalleled success.

In closing, remember that your life's journey is an exquisite canvas, and you, armed with an array of soft skills, are the artist. Paint with bold strokes of communication, subtle shades of emotional intelligence, and the vibrant colors of collaboration and adaptability. With each day that passes, you're not just living; you're crafting a masterpiece. Now, step forward with confidence, for the world awaits the story only you can write.

Appendix A:
Appendix

As we transition from the comprehensive journey through the landscape of soft skills, let's pivot to tools that will assist you in deepening your understanding and refining your abilities. The following resources are not just supplementary; they are vital instruments you can employ to continue learning, growing, and propelling yourself toward greater success.

Resources for Further Learning

Consider the wealth of knowledge waiting to be discovered as you augment your soft skills repertoire. But where to begin? With an ever-expanding universe of information at your fingertips, choosing the right resources can be an overwhelming task. To streamline your journey, we've curated a selection of stellar materials that will provide direction and inspiration.

A comprehensive list of books that dive into each soft skill with gusto, affording you the knowledge to understand the intricate workings of emotional intelligence, the subtleties of communication, and the bold strokes of leadership.

Websites and online platforms where thought leaders speak on the transformative power of soft skills in personal and professional spheres, offering tangible tips through articles, interviews, and interactive content.

Podcasts that blend the wisdom of experts with the convenience of auditory learning, enabling you to soak in insights during your commute, workout, or leisure time.

Practice Exercises for Skill Development

Knowledge without application is like an unused treasure chest – it may hold potential, but its true value remains unrealized. This section is your key to unlocking that chest. Inside, you'll find a series of exercises crafted to strengthen each soft skill through intentional practice.

Communication drills that train you to articulate your thoughts with clarity and confidence while listening with intent.

Scenarios to practice emotional intelligence, where you'll learn to navigate complex emotional landscapes both within yourself and in your interactions with others.

Teamwork challenges that encourage you to find your place within a group, harness collective strengths, and drive toward common goals together.

Remember, the cultivation of soft skills is a continuous endeavor. It's a journey filled with growth, challenges, and triumphs. Use this appendix as your compass, leading you to uncharted territories of personal development. Keep moving forward, eager to learn and ready to embrace the endless possibilities that your soft skills unlock.

Resources for Further Learning

Embarking on a voyage towards mastery of soft skills is just the start. Perhaps, our journey through the pages of this book has sparked a fresh curiosity within you – a desire to dive even deeper into the art of honing these crucial competencies. You're in luck, for there exists an abundance of resources awaiting your eager mind. Let's explore them together.

Books are an eternal fountain of knowledge, offering a world of insight into the realm of soft skills. There's a rich library of texts penned by thought leaders and experts who've delved into emotional intelligence, communication strategies, leadership, and more. Some of these books don't just instruct; they transform the way you think. Seek out works that challenge your perceptions and offer practical advice for real-world applications.

Online platforms are a treasure trove for further learning, brimming with courses that span the gamut of soft skills. Websites like Coursera, Udemy, and LinkedIn Learning provide a wealth of information through their comprehensive courses. You can learn at your own pace, test your knowledge, and gain certificates to showcase your growing proficiency. Commit to a class that resonates with your personal goals and immerse yourself in the learning experience.

If interaction and discussion ignite your passion, then webinars and workshops may be your arena for growth. These forums bring together like-minded individuals and experts for live learning experiences. They allow for immediate feedback, interactive exercises, and a chance to see how theory translates into practice in dynamic settings. Keep an eye out for events related to soft skills, and don't hesitate to participate fully.

Sometimes, the wisdom of a mentor can cast a light on the path to improvement in a way that other resources cannot. A mentor can be a guide, a coach, a sounding board for ideas, and a valuable network connection. Seek someone whose soft skills you admire and who exhibits the qualities you strive for. Whether in your field of work, study, or within local communities, mentors help weave experience into learning.

Discussion groups and forums can also serve as a rich soil for growth. Engaging with peers allows for the exchange of ideas and experiences that can illuminate different perspectives. These conversations often provide practical tips and can inspire you to test out new approaches in your everyday interactions.

Let's not forget about podcasts – these accessible nuggets of insight can accompany you during commutes, workouts, or quiet moments of reflection. Subscribing to podcasts that focus on personal development and soft skills can complement your learning process, giving you access to interviews with professionals and stories that deepen your understanding.

Blogs and articles are another resource that shouldn't be overlooked. In our fast-paced world, these often provide concise, focused overviews or deep dives into specific aspects of soft skills. They can serve as quick refreshers or introductions to new concepts. Make it a habit to follow a few well-respected blogs that consistently deliver quality content.

For a more academic approach, scholarly articles and journals delve into the science and psychology behind soft skills. They can provide evidence-based strategies and delve deeper into the intricacies of each skill set. These may be more technical but can offer a solid foundation for understanding the theoretical frameworks that underpin practice.

Educational institutions often provide community courses or adult education programs focused on personal development and professional skills. These can be valuable for those who prefer a structured classroom setting and enjoy face-to-face interaction with instructors and fellow learners.

Technology, too, offers innovative ways to practice soft skills. Try out apps and software that are designed to improve habits, support goal setting, or even simulate social interactions. Many of these tools use gamification to make learning more engaging and effective.

Video tutorials can be especially helpful for visual learners. Platforms like YouTube have countless instructional videos on every aspect of soft skills. From tips on body language to role-play scenarios, there's a plethora of content for those who learn best by watching and doing.

Don't overlook the value of conferences, either. They are not only about networking; they are also rich in seminars and breakout sessions focused on professional and personal development. Make the most out of these experiences by actively engaging with speakers and participants.

Finally, don't underestimate the power of reflection. Journals and reflection logs are simple yet powerful tools for internalizing and applying what you've learned. Write about your experiences, analyze your progress, and set new targets for your soft skill development journey.

As you continue to explore these resources, remember that the landscape of learning is continuously shifting and expanding. New opportunities for growth will emerge, and you should remain open to exploring them. Perseverance, coupled with the right resources, will guide you as you weave soft skills into the very fabric of your personal and professional life.

In summary, the path to soft skill excellence is not a solitary one; it's a shared journey. Draw upon the collective wisdom available to you, invest time in further learning, and embrace each resource as a stepping stone towards success. Remember, every interaction, every challenge, is an opportunity for growth – seize it with both hands and a willing heart.

Practice Exercises for Skill Development

As we've learned throughout this book, developing soft skills is essential for success in all walks of life. Now that we have a comprehensive understanding of the various soft skills, it's time to put that knowledge into practice. This section presents a suite of exercises designed to help you develop and refine these crucial abilities.

Think of these exercises as your personal training ground, where you are both the coach and the athlete. Each activity is crafted to challenge you, push you out of your comfort zone, and encourage growth in the soft skills that will pave the way for your accomplishments.

Let's start with communication. To sharpen your verbal skills, create a weekly journaling habit where you reflect on recent conversations. Were your points clearly articulated? Did you allow others to express themselves? This reflective practice fosters a greater awareness of how you communicate and offers insights for improvement.

For non-verbal communication, spend a day observing body language in others and in yourself. How does posture convey confidence? What signals does eye contact send? Noting these can significantly enhance your ability to read a room and respond appropriately.

Listening skills are vital, so engage in active listening during your next dialogue. Remind yourself not to interrupt, listen without planning your response, and provide feedback that shows you truly understand the speaker's message. Make this a habit to transform the way you engage with others.

Moving onto emotional intelligence, try to identify and label your emotions as they occur throughout the day. Acknowledge these feelings and ponder their impact on your interactions. Are they serving you well, or do they need managing? Emotionally intelligent people are those who understand and handle their emotions adeptly.

For honing problem-solving skills, challenge yourself with a puzzle a day, whether it be a crossword, Sudoku, or a brainteaser. The objective here is not just to find a solution, but also to examine the problem-solving strategies you employ and how they can apply to real-life scenarios.

Teamwork can be practiced in any group setting, so volunteer for a project or a committee where you can contribute and also observe group dynamics. Reflect on your role and how effectively the team collaborates. Seek to be the unifying force that drives collective success.

To develop adaptability, put yourself in a new or unexpected situation at least once a month. Reflect on how you handle the change and what you learn from it. Do you adapt swiftly or resist the unknown? The aim here is to become comfortable with the uncomfortable.

Leadership involves influence, and you can practice this by leading a small initiative or project. How do you motivate your peers? What leadership style do you naturally adopt? Leadership is about inspiring others towards a common goal, and practice will refine your approach.

Negotiation skills can be developed by simulating negotiations or role-playing with a friend or mentor. Choose a topic and argue for opposing interests. This will teach you the value of understanding different perspectives and the skill of finding a mutually beneficial resolution.

Conflicts are inevitable, which makes conflict resolution skills indispensable. Next time you encounter a disagreement, consciously employ strategies discussed in the book to find a resolution. Analyze what works and what doesn't, and note it down for future reference.

Time management is best practiced by planning your week ahead, with clear goals and priorities. At the end of the week, reflect on your productivity, what you achieved, and where your time management could be improved. Remember, time is a non-renewable resource. Use it wisely!

Networking is another key skill. At your next social or professional gathering, make it a point to introduce yourself to someone new. Strike up a conversation, find common ground, and exchange contact information. The more you practice, the more natural it becomes.

Finally, to cultivate a strong work ethic, set a personal standard for the quality of work you produce and stick to it, no matter the task at hand. Notice when you are tempted to cut corners and remind yourself of the long-term value of diligence and commitment.

Remember that the journey to improving your soft skills is ongoing. It's a path of continual development, self-discovery, and incremental progress. Use these exercises not just once, but repeatedly, as they are tools that can help sharpen your soft skills throughout all stages of life.

By engaging with these exercises regularly, they won't just prep you for hypothetical scenarios; they'll empower you to navigate the complexities and nuances of the real world with grace, confidence, and proficiency. Here's to your growth and success!